Exploring Redwood National Park

by Robert J. Dolezal

*and the Editors of
Interface California Corporation*

*Distributed by: The Touchstone Press
P.O. Box 81
Beaverton, Oregon 97005*

Geology Editor:	Steven M. Colman
Wildlife Editor:	Timothy E. Lawlor, PhD
Plantlife Editors:	James P. Smith, PhD
	John O. Sawyer, PhD
	David L. Largent, PhD
Fishing Editor:	John DeWitt, PhD
Hiking Editors:	Norman Allen
	Michelle Bertolo
	Daniel Sealy
Watercraft Editor:	Donald Banducci

Manuscript Editor:	Barbara J. Fengler
Cartography:	Genelle W. Dolezal
	Thomas Fillebrown
Layout and Design:	Peter E. Palmquist
	Robert J. Dolezal
Printing:	Graphic Arts Center, Portland, Oregon

Interface California Corporation
1806 E. Street, Suite B
Eureka, California 95501

ACKNOWLEDGMENTS

The editors and staff of Interface California Corporation express their appreciation and thanks to the many persons that made EXPLORING REDWOOD NATIONAL PARK possible. We especially thank the personnel of the National Park Service, California State Department of Parks and Recreation, Save-The-Redwoods League and Sierra Club. Each provided invaluable aid and cooperation far in excess of duty or accommodation.

The editors also wish to personally thank John H. Davis and Homer P. Leach of the National Park Service; Newton B. Drury, John B. Dewitt and Lawrence C. Merriam of Save-The-Redwoods League; Alan D. Philbrook, Herman E. Schlerf, David Redding, Nolan Albright, Terry Adams and Dana Long of California State Department of Parks and Recreation; and Dave VandeMark and Lucille Vineyard of the Sierra Club.

We were fortunate to be able to call on many individuals for aid. Especially, we acknowledge the counsel of Linda L. Finn, Stephen D. Viers, Jr., Henry W. Saddler, Jack W. Schlotter, Ken Boe, Dave Barnes, Frederick P. Cranston, Robert Wotterspoon, Richard LaForge, Barbara J. Fengler, Sharon Franco, Richard Montague, Neil Gilchrist, Ralph Perry, Robert Brett Matzke, Tom Fillebrown, Janice Schopfer, Carl Palmquist, David Swanlund, Jess Evansizer, Kent Seegmiller, Howard King, Tom Collins, Carney J. Campion, Jere Smith, Erich Schimps, Lewis Pryor, Helen Happ, Pamela Burgess, Oral Bullard, Robin Samuels, Doug Herr, Clark Mishler and Sally Palmquist.

For providing us with irreplaceable photographs of historic interest, Interface California Corporation would also like to acknowledge the aid of Humboldt State University Library and the Richard A. Childs Collection.

*To George F. Dolezal
and C. Eric Palmquist*

A portion of the proceeds of EXPLORING REDWOOD NATIONAL PARK *are donated to Save-The-Redwoods League for continued preservation of the coast redwoods.*

TABLE OF CONTENTS

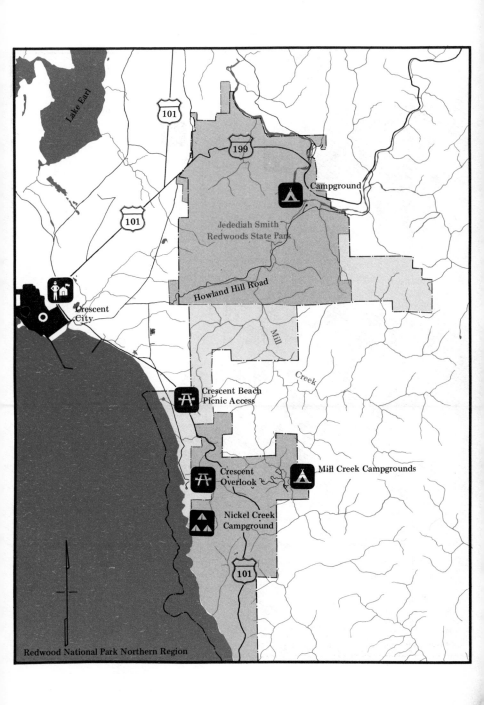

Redwood National Park Northern Region

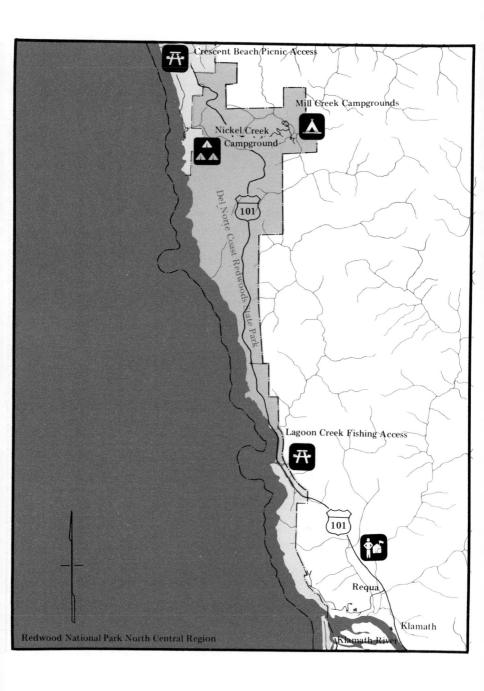

Crescent Beach/Picnic Access

Mill Creek Campgrounds

Nickel Creek Campground

Del Norte Coast Redwoods State Park

101

Lagoon Creek Fishing Access

101

Requa

Klamath

Redwood National Park North Central Region

Klamath River

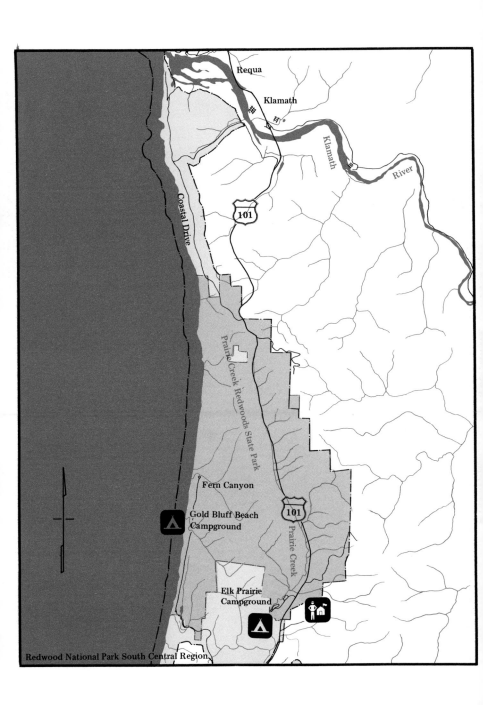

Requa

Klamath

Klamath River

Coastal Drive

101

Prairie Creek Redwoods State Park

Fern Canyon

Gold Bluff Beach Campground

101

Prairie Creek

Elk Prairie Campground

Redwood National Park South Central Region

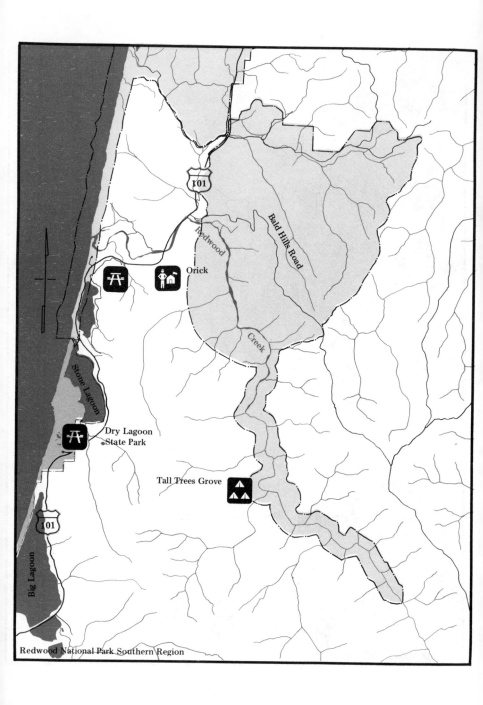

Redwood National Park Southern Region

A PARK TO EXPLORE

California's Redwood National Park is unique among parks of the National Park and Monument System. Of the 56,201 acres *(24,745 hectares)* authorized by Congress, nearly 28,430 acres *(11,506 hectares)* remain as California state park inclusions. Throughout both the federal and state lands, a gentle wilderness containing coast redwood forest, rolling hills, scenic seacoast and abundant wildlife draws to the park each year a diverse and rapidly widening number of visitors.

More than 1000 species of plants and animals occur within the park. Included among wildlife are such magnificent creatures as Roosevelt elk, black bear and deer. Beaver and porcupine feed on the tender bark of alders, while water ouzel, great blue heron and turnstones may be viewed nearby. In spring, visitors may view spectacular blooms of western azalea and California rose-bay rhododendron. Tiny orchids, colorful oxalis and star-like wake robin dot the forest floor. Towering hundreds of feet above, and unique among trees, the coast redwoods lend quiet mystery to both slopes and streamside flats.

Redwood National Park is a park to explore. Over 100 miles *(160.9 km)* of established hiking trails link visitor facilities and gateway cities with scenic coastline and forest. Three major waterways flow through the park, offering visitors fishing and recreation. Near the southern boundary, coastal lagoons provide additional opportunity for boaters, water skiers and sailors.

The editors of EXPLORING REDWOOD NATIONAL PARK believe that this guidebook will provide visitors with both immediate information and lasting enjoyment. On behalf of both the National Park Service and the California State Department of Parks and Recreation, we extend our welcome to Redwood National Park.

USING *EXPLORING REDWOOD NATIONAL PARK*

Exploring Redwood National Park offers visitors the most current and comprehensive information available on the park. Whether visitors are planning an afternoon excursion for picnicing or an extended stay of several weeks, this guidebook provides constant information to travelers.

Nine chapters cluster subjects for easy reading. Included are Gateways and Facilities, History, Geology, Climate and Weather, The Coast Redwoods, Wildlife, Plantlife, Fishing and Hiking & Watercraft Trails. Over 50 color and black & white photographs and 30 maps, with accompanying text, describe trails and facilities available to park visitors.

Each chapter is self-contained and may be read alone. For example, the chapter on Fishing provides information on best waters for angling. Visitors seeking additional information on wildlife or facilities may turn to those chapters for guidance. This editorial approach necessitates some repetition but allows travelers limited by time a more full understanding of the park.

For the convenience of both foreign and domestic readers, measurements given in the English system are followed in parenthesis by their Metric equivalents.

While the editors of *Exploring Redwood National Park* have made every attempt to eliminate factual and interpretive errors, they recognize that such mistakes may occur. Changes effected following publication are, of course, beyond editorial control. All readers are urged to aid in updating the guidebook. Suggestions or corrections for future editions should be mailed to: Interface California Corporation, 1806 E. Street, Suite B, Eureka, California 95501.

Redwood National Park and the three included state parks carry on a tradition of scenic enjoyment and recreation. The editors hope that this publication may help visitors more completely enjoy their stays in the park, and aid the park administrations in their efforts to pass on, unspoiled, the splendid wilderness of the park.

Redwood National Park was established by Congress on October 2, 1968 to aid the preservation of coast redwood forests. The park encompasses much of northwestern California, extending along the Pacific coast from its southern entrance at Orick to the northern boundary near Crescent City.

Included by Congress within national park boundaries are three California state parks: Prairie Creek Redwoods, Del Norte Coast Redwoods and Jedediah Smith Redwoods state parks. Because more than half the total 56,201.3 acres *(22,744.7 hectares)* of Congress-defined boundaries remain in California State care, most visitor facilities may be found there. Such facilities include four major campsites and picnic areas, several day-use units and more than 100 miles *(161 km)* of hiking trails.

ACCESS BY CAR/CAMPER OR MOTORHOME

From San Francisco. Visitors wishing to travel north from San Francisco to Redwood National Park by car/camper or motorhome may choose between three possible routes. Most direct is a path leading north from Golden Gate Bridge on U.S. Highway 101. Visitors should follow the highway 235 miles *(378 km)* to the southern park boundary at Orick gateway. Major communities along the route include Santa Rosa, Ukiah, Garberville, Fortuna, Eureka and Arcata. All may provide food, lodging and automobile services to travelers.

From Orick, visitors may continue north to Prairie Creek Redwoods State Park, Klamath, Requa, Del Norte Coast Redwoods State Park and Crescent City. Crescent City is the

largest community near the park and offers a wide range of visitor accommodations, lodgings, food and entertainment. From Crescent City, travelers should continue by car north on U.S. Highway 101 to its junction with U.S. Highway 199. Highway 199 leads in six miles *(9.6 km)* to Jedediah Smith Redwoods State Park, the most northerly California State Park. Beyond, visitors may continue from the park on U.S. Highway 199 to the Oregon border, Grants Pass and Interstate Highway 5.

Visitors may also follow two coastal routes north from San Francisco to the park. Although both distances are longer than the primary route, scenic views of northcoast California may prove attractive to visitors with additional time.

The shorter coastal route totals an approximate distance of 348 miles *(559.9 km)* and travels north on California State Route 1 from the Golden Gate Bridge. Visitors should continue north to Leggett, then proceed on U.S. Highway 101 134 miles *(216 km)* to the southern boundary of the park.

A longer alternate also follows Route 1 from San Francisco to Orick. Cross the Golden Gate Bridge and again proceed north on Route 1. Travel approximately 171 miles *(275 km)* to Fort Bragg and continue east an additional 35 miles *(56 km)* to Willits. From Willits, the Orick gateway is 179 miles *(288 km)* north on U.S. Highway 101. Total distance for this route is 386 miles *(621 km)*.

From Eureka. Visitors who wish to reach Redwood National Park from Eureka by car/camper or motorhome should travel north on U.S. Highway 101. The southern boundary of the park is approximately 36.5 miles *(58.7 km)* north. Other important park mileages from Eureka are: Orick, 44 miles *(70.8 km)*; Klamath, 61 miles *(19.1 km)*; Requa, 65 miles *(104 km)*; and Crescent City, 82 miles *(132 km)*.

From Portland. Visitors should follow Interstate Highway 5 south approximately 246 miles *(396 km)* to its junction with U.S. Highway 199 at Grants Pass. Enroute, travelers pass Salem, Corvalis, Eugene and Roseburg. Each community offers food, lodging and automobile service facilities to highway visitors. From Grants Pass, continue along U.S. Highway 199 to the northeast boundary of Redwood National Park, 78 miles

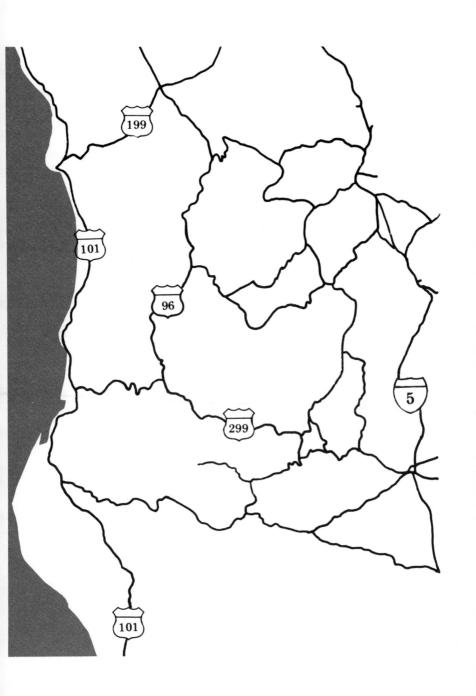

(125 km) southwest. Enroute, travelers depart Oregon and enter California. Few highway facilities for automobile service exist between Grants Pass and Crescent City, and visitors should assure an ample supply of gasoline before beginning the 104-mile *(167-km)* stretch.

Visitors approaching the park from Portland may alternately travel southwest on Oregon State Route 18, leading 87 miles *(140 km)* to Lincoln City and U.S. Highway 101. From Lincoln City, the route travels south along the Pacific seacoast to Coos Bay and Brookings, then passes into California 247 miles *(397 km)* south. Approximately 20 miles *(32.2 km)* south of the California border, visitors reach the Crescent City gateway and may proceed either east or south to Redwood National Park. Total Portland - Crescent City mileage is 334 miles *(537 km)*.

ACCESS BY MOTORCOACH

Greyhound Bus Lines offers daily motorcoach service to Redwood National Park from departure points which include San Francisco, Eureka, Crescent City and Portland. Visitors seeking information regarding bus transport to the park should contact agents of Greyhound in person or by telephone. In San Francisco, call (415) 433-1500. Buses depart daily from San Francisco to Orick and Crescent City, following the direct route via U.S. Highway 101. Travel time is approximately 9.5 hours. Round trip fare from San Francisco to Orick is $25.26, one way $13.40.

In Eureka, call (707) 442-0370. Buses depart daily from Eureka to Orick and Crescent City. Travel time is approximately one hour. Round trip fare from Eureka to Orick is $4.41, one way $2.32.

In Portland, call (503) 228-5171. Buses depart daily from Portland to Crescent City and travel time is approximately 10.5 hours. Round trip fare from Portland to Crescent City is $32.60, one way $17.15.

All fares are subject to change.

ACCESS BY AIRCRAFT

Visitors may reach Redwood National Park from many distant points by commercial jet service. At present, only one airline offers daily, scheduled jet service to gateway cities near the park. Hughes Airwest flies daily to Eureka/Arcata and Crescent City from San Francisco and Portland.

From San Francisco. Weekday flights depart three times daily from San Francisco to Eureka, non-stop. Flight time is 1 hour, 15 minutes. Round trip fare purchased in California is $60.77, one way $30.39. For reservations in San Francisco area, call (415) 397-3121.

Two flights per day leave San Francisco to Crescent City; each has one stop enroute. Round trip fare is $76.77, one way $38.39. Flight time is approximately two hours.

From Portland. Visitors in Portland seeking reservations should telephone (503) 224-5252. Flights to Crescent City from Portland leave twice daily and either make one or two stops, depending on the flight taken. Flight duration is approximately two hours. Round trip fare is $75.27, one way $37.64.

On weekdays, flights also depart four times daily from Portland to Eureka/Arcata, with one or two stops, depending on flight taken. Flight time is approximately 2 hours, 15 minutes. Round trip fare is $83.27, one way $41.64.

All rates are subject to change.

Eureka Aero Industries. Executive turboprop aircraft of Eureka Aero Industries also provide air access from San Francisco area to Redwood National Park gateway cities. Flights depart Oakland International Airport to Murray Field, north of Eureka, daily except weekends. Round trip fare from Oakland to Eureka is $52.00, one way $26.00. Equipment used is six-passenger Cessna 402 Twin. Persons seeking further information should contact:

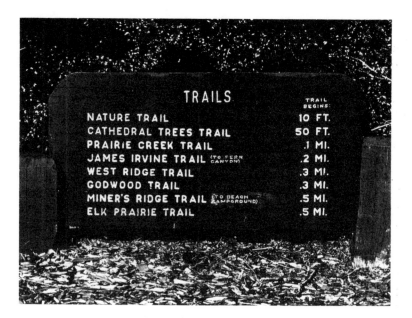

Flight Operations
Eureka Aero Industries
Murray Field
Eureka, California 95501

Telephone: (707) 443-5603

Air Charter Near Redwood National Park. Several flight services provide air charter near the park. Visitors seeking information on air charter should contact:

Flight Operations
Eureka Aero Industries
Murray Field
Eureka, California 95501

Telephone: (707) 443-5603

Flight Operations
Benbow Aero Inc.
Municipal Airport
Crescent City, California 95531

Telephone: (707) 464-4430

Flight Operations
Patton's Air Taxi
Arcata Airport
McKinleyville, California 95521

Telephone: (707) 839-2555

Car Rental. Arriving aircraft visitors to park gateway cities of Eureka/Arcata and Crescent City may wish to rent automobiles for sightseeing or travel within Redwood National Park. Several agencies operate car rental agencies offering new-model vehicles. Arriving passengers should contact, in person, by telephone, by nationwide reservation system or by writing:

In Eureka: *Avis Rent A Car*
Arcata Airport
McKinleyville, California 95521

Telephone: (707) 839-1576

Hertz Rent A Car
Arcata Airport
McKinleyville, California 95521

Telephone: (707) 839-2172

Western Car Rental
1444 Union Street
Eureka, California 95501

Telephone: (707) 443-9755

In Crescent City: *Hertz Rent A Car*
284 L. Street
Crescent City, California 95531

Telephone: (707) 464-2339

Avis Rent A Car
Crescent City Airport
Crescent City, California 95531

Telephone: (707) 464-2339

Ford Rent A Car
1105 Northcrest Drive
Crescent City, California 95531

Telephone: (707) 464-3128

Recreational Vehicle Rental.   Park air visitors arriving in Eureka/Arcata may wish to rent campers, motorhomes or trailers while near the park.   Two local agencies provide such rental:

Redwood Rentals
7th & G. Streets
Arcata, California 95521

Telephone: (707) 822-1167

Johnson's Trailer Rentals
2761 Hubbard Lane
Eureka, California 95501

Telephone: (707) 443-6600

Boat Charter. Visitors to Redwood National Park may charter boats for fishing and sightseeing at Eureka, Klamath, Requa and Smith River. Prices vary widely depending both on craft and rental agencies, and little need exists for reservations.

Travelers within the park may also explore Klamath River on jet boats. Klamath Jet Boat Kruises provides a 64-mile *(103-km)* scenic round trip excursion throughout summer visitor season. Boats depart Requa each day at 9:00 a.m., and return at 3:00 p.m., following lunch upriver. Rates for the excursion are: Adults, $6.00; children 4 - 11, $3.00; and children under age 4, no charge. During the period from June to early September, reservations are advisable. Visitors seeking either additional information or reservations should contact:

Klamath Jet Boat Kruises
Klamath, California 95548

Telephone: (707) 482-4191

VISITOR FACILITIES

Most visitor facilities found within the Congress-defined boundaries of Redwood National Park remain in administrative control of the California State Department of Parks and Recreation. Although Congress authorized inclusion of Prairie Creek Redwoods, Del Norte Coast Redwoods and Jedediah Smith Redwoods state parks when it established the park in 1968, transfer of the units has not yet occurred. In the interim period, visitors to lands within the boundary will likely make use of state, as well as national, facilities.

For the convenience of visitors, EXPLORING REDWOOD NATIONAL PARK only makes distinction between federal and state lands when clarification of regulations, fees or manage-

ment policies is necessary. For the remainder of the book, both areas are treated as contiguous park lands offering recreational enjoyment to travelers who visit.

Redwood National Park. Federal lands of Redwood National Park include blocks east and south of Crescent City, seacoast lands from False Klamath Cove south to Prairie Creek Redwoods State Park, and lands near Redwood Creek and Little Lost Man Creek. Because such lands were held in private ownership as recently as 1968, few facilities have been developed for visitors. No campsites, with exception of Nickel Creek Campground for backpackers, exist within federal lands.

Information posts, operated by personnel of the National Park Service, are located at Orick, Redwood Ranger Station and Crescent City Park Headquarters. Visitors seeking information regarding trails and day-use facilities in federal lands should contact rangers at these posts prior to use. Information may also be obtained by writing or telephoning park headquarters in Crescent City:

Superintendent
Redwood National Park
P.O. Drawer N
Crescent City, California 95531

Telephone: (707) 464-6101

Orick Seacoast. Visitors entering Redwood National Park from the south first contact park boundaries while descending to Orick Beach, located 4.4 miles *(7.1 km)* west of Orick on U.S. Highway 101. The beach has no developed facilities operated by the National Park Service, but a small Humboldt County Park provides limited day-use facilities near the mouth of Redwood Creek.

Orick. Orick *(population 650)*, is the southernmost community closely adjacent Redwood National Park. An information post, operated by personnel of the National Park Service is located immediately north of U.S. Highway 101 bridge spanning Redwood Creek. Orick offers limited visitor facilities, including

Land and sea meet here, wi...
into the misty distance.

This beach, known as Gold Bluf...
six miles. It's attractions include ...
Elk, Fern Canyon, and an expans...
Access is by way of Davison Road, ...
Orick, off Highway 101.

tural beach stretches

xtends more than
erd of Roosevelt
f sandy beach.
miles north of

motel accommodations, restaurants, sporting goods and auto-mobile service. The town also provides access to Bald Hills Road, location of Lady Bird Johnson Grove, and Redwood Creek, site of the tallest known coast redwood. A road leading west from the community along the north bank of Redwood Creek provides backpacker access to Mussel Point Beach, the terminus of Gold Bluff Beach-Redwood Creek Hike.

Bald Hills Road. Trailers and motorhomes are not advised on this steep, narrow access to Lady Bird Johnson Grove, located 1.4 miles *(2.2 km)* north of Orick on U.S. Highway 101. A parking access is located .8 mile *(1.2 km)* east of the junction, and provides visitors parking for towed vehicles. The parking access is the starting point of Redwood Creek Hike, leading in eight miles *(12.8 km)* to Tall Trees Grove, site of the tallest known coast redwood, the Howard A. Libby, or Tall Tree. Tall Tree stretches 367.8 feet *(112.1 m)* from its base near Redwood Creek. Approximately 2.8 miles *(4.5 km)* from junction with U.S. Highway 101, a second parking access and pedestrian bridge provide entry to Lady Bird Johnson Grove, dedication point of the park. On November 25, 1968, Mrs. Johnson, ac-companied by her husband and President Richard M. Nixon, dedicated the park in a ceremony lasting nearly two hours. A self-guided nature walk for those with additional time offers the opportunity to acquaint oneself with coast redwood forest. Visitors traveling Bald Hills Road should take care to avoid dangerous parking or roadside walking. Large commercial vehicles travel the road throughout the year, making such travel hazardous.

Coastal Drive. Coastal Drive, an eight-mile *(12.9-km)* alternate to U.S. Highway 101 follows the rugged Pacific Coast from a point 20.9 miles *(33.6 km)* north of Orick to the highway bridge spanning Klamath River. Enroute, visitors may examine several interpretive plaques describing geologic features, Indian legends, and wildlife of the park seacoast. The Coastal Drive also provides access to start of Gold Bluff Beach-Redwood Creek Hike, Alder Conservation Camp, and a walk leading to Split Rock. Towed vehicles are not advised for traveling much of the route.

Klamath and Klamath Glen. Located 25.5 miles *(41 km)* north of Orick on U.S. Highway 101, Klamath *(population 200)* and Klamath Glen *(population 300)* provide a wide range of visitor accommodations, including lodging, food services, boat rental, sanitary system disposal, automobile service and a convenience store. The communities also provide access to waters of Klamath River, popular among fishermen for its large summer and autumn runs of steelhead and salmon.

Requa. Located 1.8 miles *(2.9 km)* north of Klamath, Requa *(population 150)* offers visitor accommodations, food and lodging. Boat rentals for fishing the mouth of Klamath River, and scenic jet boat cruises upriver 32 miles *(51.5 km)* to Martins Ferry may be arranged in Requa. The community also provides entry to Klamath Air Force Station, a radar facility, and is a starting point for the Coastal Hike, leading in 4.3 miles *(6.9 km)* to False Klamath Cove.

Redwood Ranger Station. Personnel of Redwood Ranger Station, located 1.8 miles *(2.9 km)* north of Requa, may provide visitors with both information regarding park federal lands and evening interpretive programs during summer visitor season. Such programs are held each Thrusday at 7:30 p.m. and are free to the traveling public.

Trees of Mystery Area. Between Redwood Ranger Station and Lagoon Creek Fishing Access, located 5.5 miles *(8.8 km)* north of Klamath River highway bridge, numerous private operators have established commercial businesses providing visitor accommodations, lodging, food, automobile service and sightseeing attractions. Included is *Trees of Mystery*, offering visitors a self-guided walk describing many features of coast redwood forest, souvenirs and an Indian museum.

Lagoon Creek-False Klamath Cove. U.S. Highway 101 parallels closely the Pacific Ocean at the mouth of Wilson Creek, located 5.5 miles *(8.8 km)* north of Klamath River highway bridge. National Park Service facilities at Wilson Creek/False Klamath

Cove include beach access, a self-guided interpretive walk, picnicing, fishing, and is the terminus of the Coastal Hike from Requa. Lagoon Creek Fishing Access facilities include picnic tables and chemical toilets.

Enderts Beach Road. Located two miles *(3.2 km)* south of Crescent City, Enderts Beach Road junctions with U.S. Highway 101. The road provides access to two day-use facilities, Crescent Beach Picnic Area and Crescent Beach Overlook. Crescent Beach Picnic Area provides picnic tables, running water, barbecue pits and chemical toilets. Crescent Beach Overlook offers picnic tables and barbecue pits, but no toilets or running water. Enderts Beach Road terminates on a bluff overlooking the Pacific Ocean, the start of a .5-mile *(.8-km)* trail leading to Nickel Creek Campground. The campground has no road access and is intended solely for backpacker use. Space for 15-20 persons is provided, and pit toilets complete the facility. Nickel Creek empties nearby into waters of the Pacific Ocean at Enderts Beach. The campground terminates Nickel Creek-Last Chance Hike, which starts at Damnation Creek.

Crescent City. Crescent City *(population 15,000)*, located 275 miles *(442 km)* north of San Francisco and 340 miles *(547 km)* south of Portland, is the headquarters city for Redwood National Park. Visitors may obtain park information at the headquarters building, 1111 Second Street. Crescent City provides a wide range of visitor accommodations, including lodging, food, vehicle service and private campsites suitable for both campers and recreational vehicles. It is serviced twice daily by aircraft of Hughes Airwest, motorcoaches of Greyhound Bus Lines, and is situated prominently on U.S. Highway 101, five miles *(8 km)* south of its junction with U.S. Highway 199.

CALIFORNIA STATE PARKS

State Park Reservations. Visitors intending overnight camping in units of the California State Park System must obtain reservations from Ticketron, service agent for the parks. Such reservations may be placed as much as 30 days in advance and

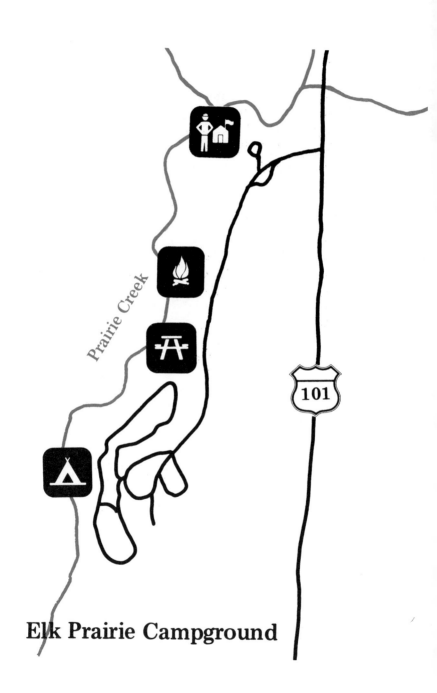

Prairie Creek

101

Elk Prairie Campground

may be made in person at agents of Ticketron, or by writing:

Ticketron
5161 W. Imperial Highway
Inglewood, California 90304

No Ticketron reservations may be made by telephone. Reservations cost $1.50 per stay and may be canceled for an additional $1.50 service charge. Rebooking a stay requires an initial booking fee of $1.50, an additional $1.50 to cancel and a second $1.50 charge to rebook. All Ticketron fees are additional to normal campsite fees charged by the California State Department of Parks and Recreation. Fees applicable to users of state park facilities are: $3.00 per night per vehicle; $1.00 for each additional vehicle; $1.00 for picnicers, and $.50 for dogs. Time limits for camping vary between the individual units.

Prairie Creek Redwoods State Park. Prairie Creek Redwoods is the most southerly state park included in the Congress-defined boundaries of Redwood National Park. It is located 5.5 miles *(8.8 km)* north of Orick, with headquarters at Elk Prairie Campground. Facilities offered include two year-round campsites, picnic areas, scenic accesses and a wide system of hiking trails, suitable for both casual and experienced backcountry travelers. Visitors seeking information regarding Prairie Creek Redwoods State Park should contact personnel of the park administration, in person, by telephone or by writing:

Area Manager
Prairie Creek Redwoods State Park
Orick, California 95555

Telephone: (707) 488-2171

Two campgrounds, Elk Prairie and Gold Bluff Beach, provide 100 campsites for visitor use. Time limitations on stay in both areas are 15 days in summer, 30 days winter. Elk Prairie Campground offers numerous rustic facilities to park visitors, including picnic tables, food storage caches, flush toilets and showers.

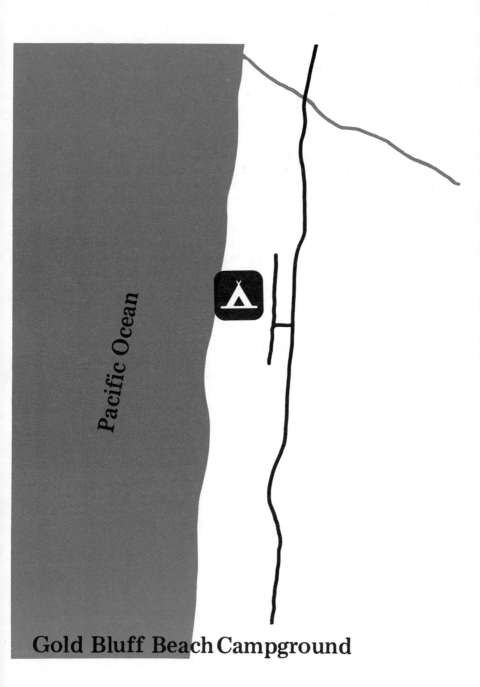

Pacific Ocean

Gold Bluff Beach Campground

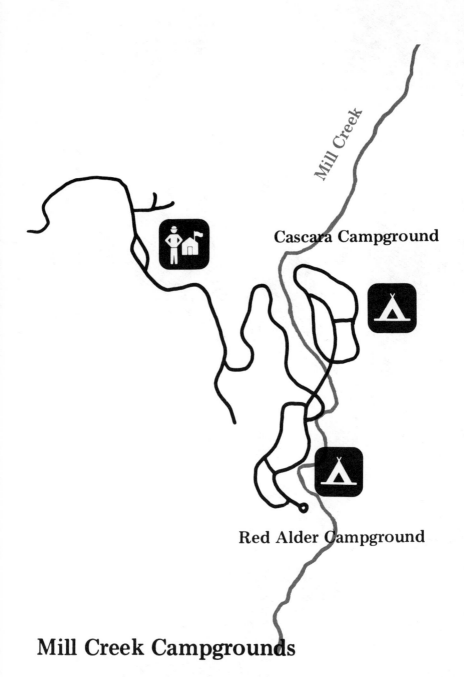

Mill Creek

Cascara Campground

Red Alder Campground

Mill Creek Campgrounds

During summer visitor season, a regular program of interpretive walks, campfire gatherings and ranger talks are provided. Visitors wishing to participate in such programs should request information at park headquarters.

Gold Bluff Beach Campground, located on Davison Road west of U.S. Highway 101, may be reached by visitors to Prairie Creek Redwoods State Park by driving 3.5 miles (5.6 km) south from Elk Prairie Campground to Davison Road turnoff. The road is marked with a signpost indicating access to Fern Canyon. Davison Road is a Humboldt County roadway and is restricted to vehicles or combinations less than seven feet (2.1 m) wide and 20 feet (6.1 m) long. These limitations are enforced by officers of the Humboldt County Sheriffs Office. Gold Bluff Beach Campground is located at the mouth of Squashan Creek, in an area of sandy beach and high bluffs. Twenty-five campsites are available to visitors, and facilities include picnic tables, food storage caches, running water and flush toilets. Visitors may collect driftwood for use as firewood, or purchase firewood at Elk Prairie headquarters for $1.00.

Del Norte Coast Redwoods State Park. Located in the central region of the Congress-defined park, Del Norte Coast Redwoods State Park offers 145 campsites in Mill Creek Campground at streamside. The campground is divided into the northern, or Cascara, unit and the southern, or Red Alder, unit. Camp facilities include tables, food storage caches, showers, toilets, laundry facilities, running water and provisions for disposal of trailer and recreational vehicle sanitary systems. A regular program of interpretive walks and talks are conducted during summer visitor season. Both facilities have camping duration limitations of 15 days.

Mill Creek Campground is closed during winter months, when personnel of the park administration move to area headquarters at Jedediah Smith Redwoods State Park. For additional information regarding facilities offered at Del Norte Coast Redwoods State Park, visitors should contact, in person, personnel of the

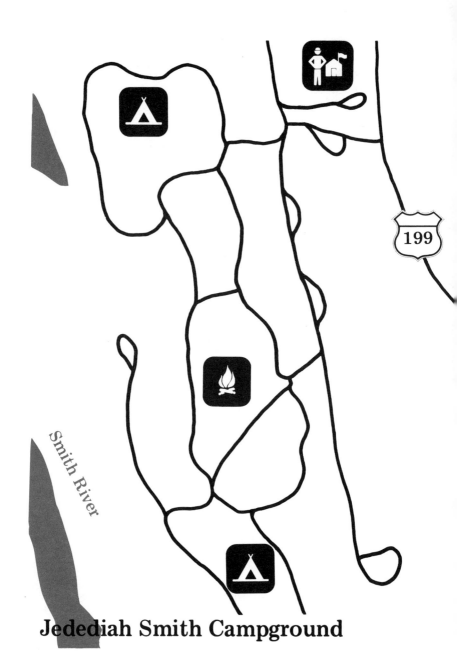

Smith River

Jedediah Smith Campground

park administration, or write:

Area Manager
Del Norte Coast Redwoods State Park
Route 2, Box 286
Crescent City, California 95531

Telephone: (707) 458-3115

Jedediah Smith Redwoods State Park. Jedediah Smith Redwoods State Park is the most northerly California State Park proposed for inclusion in Redwood National Park by Congress. Park headquarters and a campground are located 10.3 miles *(16.6 km)* northeast of the Crescent City gateway on U.S. Highway 199. Visitors from Grants Pass, Oregon first enter park boundaries at the community of Hiouchi.

The campground, situated on the banks of Smith River, provides easy summer access to Frank D. Stout Grove. Within Stout Grove grows the largest known coast redwood, Frank D. Stout Tree. It is 20 feet *(6.1 m)* in diameter at chest height. Campground facilities include 108 campsites equipped with tables, food storage caches, running water, flush toilets, laundry facilities and showers. A time limit of 10 days for campers exists from June through September. For the remainder of the year, visitors may stay in the campground without time limit. Convenience stores that offer a wide range of common items, including food, fishing tackle, ice, propane, and gasoline are located nearby at Hiouchi and west of the park near U.S. Highway 101.

Regular interpretive walks and ranger talks are conducted during summer visitor season. Campfire programs are held nightly without charge at 8:00 p.m. at the campfire center. Visitors wishing to participate in such programs should check at park headquarters for current schedules.

Travelers seeking additional information regarding Jedediah Smith Redwoods State Park should contact personnel of the park administration, or write:

Area Manager
Jedediah Smith Redwoods State Park
Route 2, Box 286
Crescent City, California 95531

Telephone: (707) 458-3115

PRIVATE VISITOR FACILITIES

Many commercial campgrounds, visitor facilities, motels, hotels and restaurants provide services near the park to visitors. Visitors wishing information regarding commercial operators near the park should contact:

In Humboldt County: *Chamber of Commerce*
2112 Broadway Avenue
Eureka, California 95501

Telephone: (707) 442-3738

In Del Norte County: *Chamber of Commerce*
Highway 101 North
Crescent City, California 95531

Telephone: (707) 464-3174

HISTORY

Redwood National Park lies within an area rich with history. In earliest times, Native Americans of the region lived near streams flowing through rugged mountains and redwood forest. First European explorers reached the area in 1542, but for nearly 200 years, little was known of northern California and the area surrounding Klamath River. Only in 1828, when veteran explorer and mountain man Jedediah Smith fought his way to the Pacific Ocean through dense coastal forest, were the lands within Redwood National Park opened to trappers and settlers.

Visitors to the park may easily visit historic sites spanning many years of park history. Within its boundaries, one may see both Native Americans performing dances which originated thousands of years ago, and corduroy stagecoach roads from early days that linked the Crescent City gateway with southern Oregon. Throughout the park, early roads, dwellings, and camps used for forestry and mining are common.

Early Names. Redwood National Park was named by Congress in 1968 in description of its most prominent feature: Streamside and slope groves of coast redwood forest. Most other names of the region, however, date to much earlier Indian and white settler names. Klamath River was originally described by Native Americans living near its headwaters as *Tlamatl*, the Chinook name for a sister tribe of Modoc Indians. Usage over many years gradually altered the name to its present form. Crescent City was named in 1853 by its founder, J. F. Wendell, for the moon-shaped bay stretching southward from Point Saint George. In earlier times, it was called Paragon Bay. The Orick gateway was named for Indians living along Redwood Creek, prior to arrival of first white men. They were called *Oruk*. The town of Requa owes its name to its village chief, *Rech-wa*, whose name meant creek-mouth in California Yurok dialect. The nearby community of Klamath Glen was called *Ter-Waw* in early days, taken from the native village and later United States Army fort, erected on the spot.

The origin of many place names are clouded by spoken history and legends. Native Americans living near the mouth of Klamath River in the central park relate the following legend regarding their home:

Before the world that we know came to be, there were only spirits of the air.. The greatest of all ruled over this world of ghosts, even as he does today. His name was called Wah-Pec-oo-May-ow. He decided that the time had come to complete the real world, populating it with people, redwood trees, rocks, rivers and great oceans. Calling inhabitants of the other world together, he told them that they may choose to be whatever they wished to become.

Te Pah chose to stand atop seaside bluffs cooled by the ocean as the great spruce tree. Ka-Ha-Mis became the water spirit, living in rivers near the sea. But greatest of all to the Yurok Indians is Oregos, who became the rock, north of Klamath River mouth.

Oregos was a woman-spirit who wished to aid people of the new world. Because of this, Wah-Peck-oo-May-ow described to her the good she would do if she became the jagged rock near Klamath; its creeks and streams and tributaries. She would know where the water was cool and good, or warm and sickly. She would become guardian of the salmon runs and would guide them safely upstream each year, past shallows filled with logs or debris and around hungry animals of the shore, such as grizzly and black bear. Because she would know when the good rains would fall, she could tell the steelhead when to begin upstream. No matter regarding Klamath River was to be beyond her powers.

Wah-Peck-oo-May-ow also knew, however, that Oregos' legs would have to rise up to stretch occasionally. At such times, her legs would cross to her sister on the other bank, blocking the river waters and forcing its mouth to the south side of the spit. There it would remain, until her sister also grew tired,

crying out for relief. From the south shore, the mouth would once again move to the north.

Oregos would become the guardian of the living, and Indians wishing to spare her grief would avoid passing dead relatives near her sight when bringing them home by sea. Instead, they would beach their redwood canoes in a cove to the north and carry the corpse overland to villages inland. For such consideration, Oregos replenished the runs of salmon, steelhead and eels each year, providing food and good life.

With great happiness, Oregos heard the talk of Wah-Peck-oo-May-ow, and chose to become the rock. Each year as the salmon gather in the river mouth to begin their long runs upstream, Indians living near the river mouth say that they can be heard repeating her name in crashing of the ocean surf. They know that they are saying goodbye to the kindly Oregos for the last time, for salmon always die after spawning.

PREHISTORY

Before the first European explorers came to lands of Redwood National Park, Native Americans of three separate cultures lived within its boundaries. Because they spoke different languages, later explorers and settlers divided them into three tribes: Yurok, Tolowa and Chilula. For the natives, however, no such divisions existed, and they lacked even words to describe their nations.

Only rarely did Indians of the park venture into nearby, game-barren, coast redwood forests. Instead, they relied upon bountiful waters of the rivers and ocean for food and developed large villages on floodplains near the sea. Visitors to Redwood National Park may visit such native communities at Klamath, Requa and Redwood Creek.

The Yurok. Most numerous among Native Americans living within the park were Indians of the Yurok tribe. They lived along Klamath River for many miles inland, as well as north and

south along the seacoast. Their civilization is believed by historians to once have been the highest level attained by known groups of native Californians. Yuroks lived in sturdy plank houses built of split redwood. Such homes were warm and dry, even during long periods of extended rain. Their arts included basketry, wood carving and delicate chipped blades of stone. Even everyday items were beautifully decorated with geometric patterns depicting nearby animals of the forest or fish.

Because the Yurok lived near park rivers and streams, they were a people of the water. When asked directions by early settlers, they had no words for north, south, east or west. Instead, everything was described as upstream or downstream by the Indians.

Indians of the Yurok tribe constructed large canoes from fallen redwood logs, carefully burning and scraping the interior until finished. Such canoes were highly maneuverable, and even crashing rapids of Klamath River could be run by skillful paddlers. Because they were round-bottomed, they could easily be swung by strong strokes of the helmsman. While running rapids, rocks were often approached head-on, then shot within touching distance by those inside. Although Yurok Indians sometimes took their dugout canoes to sea, they were unsuited to such travel. Their paddles were designed for river use, and were stout poles six feet (1.8 m) or more in length. Such long paddles frequently required natives to remain standing while poling through shallow areas.

Because fish were so important to natives of Klamath River, the best riffles and holes were often protected by claims. In some cases, several Indians would jointly own a stretch of river, using it in rotation for more than 24 hours at a stretch. If a man allowed another to use his fishing spot, he received the bulk of the catch. It was forbidden to establish new fishing areas or to fish below the claim of another man.

Most salmon were caught by means of dip nets, long baskets of woven fiber, weighted with rocks and held over the river with a long pole. Native Americans of the park also speared fish, however, and frequently caught them by using community weirs.

Although the Yurok Indians relied heavily upon the river and sea for food, they also gathered acorns and seeds from inland areas. Deer and elk were caught by natives disguised in carefully prepared skins which helped them to approach these animals closely. In times of famine, even grasshoppers, angleworms, yellow-jacket larvae and yellow slugs were used for food. Only reptiles and dogs were never eaten. The Yurok believed such animals were poisonous.

Little mixing occurred among people of different Yurok communities. Indians of the region did not travel great distances, and it was not unusual for a man to die without traveling more than 25 miles *(40.2 km)* from his birthplace. Strangers were looked upon with suspicion, and natives frequently ambushed or killed them. Little difference existed in their mind between murder and war.

In times of war, the Yurok were fierce fighters who demanded compensation for any wrong. Every man injured or killed, every woman or child held hostage, and every piece of seized property must be paid for in kind, or according to its value. No quarrel ended until both sides had been fully compensated for wrongs done them. In some cases, rich natives could avoid bloodshed by paying the injured man his damages in shell money. Those not involved quietly kept their distance, even if fighting broke out in a house nearby.

The Tolowa. Living north of the Yurok tribe were the Tolowa Indians. These natives are linked closely with the Indians of southern Oregon and lived in drainages of Smith River. Their language was a dialect of Athabascan, and researchers believe their ancestors may have migrated many thousands of years ago to northern California from such far-away places as Alaska or Russia. When first explorers asked their names, they replied, *"Ni-Tolowo,"* meaning I speak Athabascan of the Tolowa variety. From this description, the tribe acquired its present name.

Many settlements of Tolowa Indians existed near the mouth of Smith River and present-day Crescent City. They followed a lifestyle similar to that of the nearby Yurok, gaining most of their food from the rivers and sea, dwelling in homes built below ground of split redwood, and constructing canoes. In art, however, they were not as advanced as the Yurok. Only their ceremonial robes and knives showed the delicate worksmanship found on many Yurok implements.

Among their customs, the Tolowa held beautiful ceremonial dances using white deerskins. Such skins were rare, and an Indian would trade his entire belongings for one. The dancers wore aprons of skunk or deer about their waists, with hanging necklaces of shell money and forehead bands of wolf fur. Large feathers, usually of eagle or condor, rose above their heads on a wooden stick, while scalps of woodpecker completed the head-dress. Above their head, the dancers held stuffed deer heads, usually white or light gray, and covered their shoulders with robes of white skins and dangling legs.

The men formed a long row, swaying and stamping in time to the song of a chanter. On each end, two dancers held long, obsidian knives of stone and wore a headdress of sea lion teeth. They crossed in front of the line of background dancers, crouching, blowing whistles and holding out their knives. The men painted their faces with thin lines of soot, blackened their jaws and striped their shoulders. Visitors to Redwood National Park may see such dances at local festivals held each year at Requa, near the mouth of Klamath River.

The Chilula. Like all Indian groups found within Redwood National Park, the Chilula lacked a name for themselves as a group. Their name was given them by first white settlers of Redwood Creek and was drawn from their word, *Tsulu-la*, or Bald Hills. Locally, they have always been known as the Bald Hills Indians. In times of war, Chilula allied against the Yurok with native groups.

Like nearly all Native Americans of the region, the Chilula built elaborate sweat houses of redwood that were used by men of the tribe. Such houses were smaller than dwellings and were planked with split redwood below ground. The timbers were tightly chinked, and only a tiny door allowed entry and exit. Within the sweat house, as many as seven men would lie around a small fire, smoking, eating, sleeping or meditating in the intense heat and smoke. During ceremonial times, many men would crowd such houses prior to dancing.

Visitors to Redwood National Park may view at Requa a reconstructed native home. The dwelling was built by members of Del Norte Historical Society at the site of a former dwelling. Those who wish to visit this native home should follow Requa Road, a turnoff located 2.7 miles *(4.3 km)* north of Klamath River highway bridge on U.S. Highway 101. Other sites nearby include Otmekor, a short distance upstream on Klamath River, and Oruk Lagoon Camp, reached by following an access road west from the Orick gateway along the north bank of Redwood Creek. Both sites are in poor repair, however, and visitors may only see excavations of former dwellings.

SEACOAST EXPLORATION

Early seacoast explorers of Redwood National Park played an important role in forming the history of the region. In earliest times, the exploration of northern California promised new lands for Spain and England. In later years, merchant voyagers and traders searched the coast for furs. Even though most seamen had only brief contact with the area, their impressions guided and excited overland explorers who finally opened the area to settlement, forestry and mining. Visitors to park seacoasts may easily understand the difficulty these rocky, inhospitable shores must have presented to men of the sea.

The Cabrillo-Ferrelo Exploration. Juan Rodriquez Cabrillo and Bartolome Ferrelo are generally given credit for being the first European explorers to attempt exploration of seacoasts near Redwood National Park. Cabrillo was Portugese by birth and a master mariner. He sailed in June, 1542 from the port of Navidad in New Spain with two ships, but died the following January from injuries sustained in a fall on San Miguel, one of the Channel Islands of southern California. His chief pilot, Bartolome Ferrelo, assumed command of Cabrillo's ships and continued northward along the California coast. Many historians believe Ferrelo passed beyond what is now the northern boundary of California to about Rogue River in southern Oregon. At no time, however, did he closely approach shore and seldom saw anything to the east except hazy mountains. On February 28, 1543, Ferrelo and his men reached the most northern point of his voyage. An account of the day related the events:

They ran this night to the west-northwest with great difficulty, and on Thursday, in the morning, the wind shifted to the southwest with great fury, the seas coming from many directions, causing them great fatigue and breaking over the ships; and as they had no decks, if God had not succored them they could not have escaped. Not being able to lay-to, they were forced to scud northeast toward land; and now, thinking themselves lost, they commended themselves to Our Lady of Guadalupe and made their vows...to make a pilgrimage to her church, naked...Thus they ran until three o'clock in the afternoon, with great fear and travail, because they concluded that they were about to be lost, for they saw many signs that the land was nearby, both birds and very green trees, which came from some rivers, although because the weather was very dark and cloudy the land was invisible. At this hour, the Mother of God succored them, by the grace of her Son, for a very heavy rainstorm came up from the north which drove them south with foresails lowered all night and until sunset the next day; and as there was a high sea from the south, it broke every time over the prow and swept over them as over a rock. The wind shifted to the northwest...with great fury, forcing them to scud to the southeast.

Driven southward by the gale, Ferrelo and his men found

themselves on March 5 once again offshore the Channel Islands. Discouraged, they returned to New Spain.

Sir Francis Drake. Sir Francis Drake, an English privateer aboard his ship, *Golden Hind*, is believed by many researchers to be the first explorer to land near the park. In 1579, Drake plundered several Spanish towns, then circled South America through the Straits of Magellen and sailed north. Near Redwood National Park, he encountered headwinds and long days of coastal fog which halted his progress.

Because few records remain of Drake's voyage, historians are uncertain of his landfalls. One map, drawn by a member of the crew, greatly resembles the coastline south of the park near Trinidad. Researchers speculate that the bay may have provided an anchorage to his ship, which was leaking badly and in great need of repair. More than 200 years later, coastal explorer Bruno de Heceta found natives of Trinidad using iron knives which may have been given to them by members of Drake's party.

Sebastian Rodriquez Cermeno. Close on the heels of Sir Francis Drake, Sebastian Rodriquez Cermeno was sent by Spain to reconnoiter the shores of northern California by ship. Because numerous Spanish vessels sailing to and from Manila had been captured or sunk by the English, Cermeno was ordered to find California ports suitable for hiding Spanish galleons. He put to sea in July, 1595.

The following November, Cermeno made landfall off the northern coast of California. Many experts who have studied his accounts believe he was near Trinidad. Many jagged rocks could be seen, however, and he continued southward along the coast. Near Drake's Bay, a short distance north from San Francisco, his ship ran aground. Cermeno and his shipmates escaped the beached hulk in a launch and reached Acapulco following several weeks of hardship.

Sebastian Vizcaino. In 1602, Sebastian Vizcaino became the last of the early seacoast explorers of northern California. He sailed northward from Acapulco to Cape San Lucas with three ships, *San Diego*, *Santo Tomas* and *Tres Reyes*. Because of sickness aboard, however, the *Santo Tomas* returned a short time later to New Spain.

In January of 1603, Vizcaino reached Cape Mendocino. A great storm separated his ships, and Vizcaino believed *Tres Reyes* had been lost. In reality, the ship had been driven north, nearly offshore Point Saint George and present-day Crescent City. Because much of her crew was ill, little exploration was possible, and the ship turned southward in hopes of rejoining Vizcaino aboard San Diego. As they sailed down the coast, they came to a large river which was flooding. With full sails and wind astern, they fought to enter it, but were unable to force their way more than six miles *(9.6 km)* upstream.

Swollen rivers are common during winter in northcoast California, and researchers believe that the powerful stream described by Vizcaino may have been Eel River. During times of flood, the river spreads more than three miles *(4.8 km)* wide and is choked with debris. From sea, it might easily be mistaken for a bay.

Again turning south, the crew of *Tres Reyes* passed Cape Mendocino, which they described as a place protected from the northwest wind by many mountains and trees. To the storm-tossed sailors, the country a few miles inland appeared pleasant and fertile.

Bodega and Heceta. Despite the meager quantity of knowledge gained by early explorers of northern California, nearly 175 years passed before ships once again sailed waters near Redwood National Park. During this period, wars occupied both Spanish and English fleets. In about 1770 the threat of Russian traders operating within Spanish territory renewed interest in northcoast California exploration. Juan Francisco de la Bodega y Cuadra and Bruno de Heceta were chosen by the Spanish governor to sail north. They departed San Blas in the summer of 1775 with two ships, but adverse winds soon forced them many miles offshore. Approaching Cape Mendocino, Bodega ordered his chief pilot to steer a course near land.

On the ninth day of June...we saw, with greatest clearness, the plains, rocks, bays, headlands, breakers and trees. At the same time we sailed along the coast, and endeavored to find out a port, being at the distance of only a mile, and approaching to a high cape, which seemed to promise shelter...many small islands concealed from us some rocks, which scarcely appeared above the surface of the sea.

A short time later, the schooner dropped anchor in calm waters protected by a lofty headland.   Like Drake and Cermeno, Bodega had found his way to Trinidad Bay, the only sheltered point obvious from sea for many miles.   Yurok Indians from a small village near the bay swarmed to the ship to trade skins, baskets and dried fish.

The Spaniards remained at Trinidad for 10 days. On Trinity Sunday they ascended the rocky headland providing shelter to their vessel.   After posting guards to protect themselves from possible Indian attack, they marched in two columns to its highest point and celebrated mass.   Because of the Roman Catholic Holy Day, they named the bay *Puerto de la Trinidad.* A cross was raised, and the territory was claimed for Spain.

After exploring nearby Little and Mad rivers, they recorded in their log a description of the *"very large, high, and straight pines, amongst which...(were) observed some of 120 feet high and four feet in diameter towards the bottom."* The unusual trees, of course were coast redwood.

George Vancouver.   George Vancouver, a British sea captain sailing from the Hawaiian Islands in April, 1792 became the next sea explorer to visit northern California.   Making landfall near Cape Mendocino, he proceeded northward along the coast and may be the first explorer to have closely examined lands within Redwood National Park.

The shores became straight and compact, not affording the slightest shelter; and lathough rising gradually from the water's edge to a moderate height only, yet the distant interior country was composed of mountains of great elevations; before which were presented a great variety of hills and dales, agreeably interspersed with woodlands and clear spots, as if in a state of cultivation; but we could discern neither houses, huts, smokes, nor other signs of its being inhabited.

Don Francisco de Eliza.   Also visiting northcoast California in 1793, Spanish commander Don Francisco de Eliza departed San Blas in April, seeking to explore Columbia River with his two vessels, *Activa* and *Mexicanna.*   Eliza was unable to proceed

further than mid-Oregon and turned south. Passing the coast of
Redwood National Park, he paused for a short time in Trinidad
Bay. After taking on water and wood, he continued southward,
hoping to reach San Francisco. His log describes the stop:

August, I succeeded in anchoring in Puerto de Trinidad...
Puerto de Trinidad is quite small; no vessel can be moored so as
to turn with the wind or tide. The bottom for the most part is
rock. The land consists of quite high and extended hills full of
pines and oaks. All kinds of fish are scarce. The settlement in
the port consists of four small houses of prepared timber. By a
piece of sawed timber we ascertained that Captain Vancouver
had been there, his men, so the Indians told us, having sawed it.
All the coast explored is inhabited by heathen...No one was
seen to bring fish nor to have fishing tackle, no doubt because
of the ferocity of the surf on the coast. We gave them hooks,
explaining by signs how to use them, but they threw them
away, giving us to understand that they were of no use.

With the visit of Eliza, early seacoast exploration of lands
near Redwood National Park ended. In years which followed,
ships of exploration yielded to tradesmen seeking furs. In
1806, Jonathan Winship, an American employed by the Russian
American Company, discovered Humboldt Bay while exploring
the coast for sea otter. Knowledge of its deep, safe harbor
remained locked in Russian documents for many years, however, and only after overland explorers entered the area did
settlers begin use of the port.

No landfalls of early seacoast explorers are known to exist
within park boundaries, but visitors may easily view Trinidad
Bay, located 16.9 miles *(27.2 km)* south of the park on U.S.
Highway 101. By following signs leading to the harbor, a
memorial lighthouse dedicated to those lost at sea also may be
seen. Visitors should then proceed to the base of the headland,
where a short, narrow road leads to a parking area atop its
bluff. From this parking area, one may either visit the current
lighthouse facility of the United States Coast Guard, or walk a
short trail to a replica of the cross dedicated by Bodega during
his expedition in 1775. Excellent views extending as far south
as Cape Mendocino on clear days may be had from this vantage
point.

OVERLAND EXPLORATION AND SETTLEMENT

A new wave of explorers soon ventured into lands near Redwood National Park. While searching for furs, new land and gold, trappers and adventurers opened wilderness trails throughout the region. The first of such mountain men was Jedediah Smith, an American trapper of the Missouri Fur Company.

Jedediah Smith. In April, 1828, Jedediah Smith led west towards Redwood National Park a party of 20 men and nearly 300 horses and mules. They departed a camp near present-day Red Bluff, located in the central valley of California. After losing a few horses to Indians living in mountains of the Trinity Alps, Smith's party reached Trinity River and began following its course downstream. Because most of the livestock were half wild, their progress was slow. Frequently horses crowded together, making movement difficult. At other times, they rushed headlong through narrow openings and were unable to continue after as little as one mile *(1.6 km)*. In areas of high elevation, snowdrifts three *(.9 m)* to four feet *(1.2 m)* deep frequently required long detours.

As the trappers struggled downstream, the familiar, short-haired natives, common to the Sacramento Valley gave way to long-haired Indians clad in buckskin, carrying axes of the Hudson's Bay Company. Their homes were small lodges that sunk halfway beneath ground and had peaks of split wood. They spoke a language unfamiliar to the whites and were unable to give Smith and his men directions to the sea.

Discouraged at their slow progress, the party sent scouts west, hoping to find a shortcut through the dense forest. These men quickly returned with news that the seacoast was less than 20 miles *(32 km)* away. Despite poor weather that hampered visibility, and poor health caused by inadequate food, Smith turned west from Trinity River towards the nearby ocean.

After several days of fair progress, they camped on May 19, 1828, atop a high ridge covered with fir, spruce and coast redwood. Looking to the west, the men saw waters of the Pacific Ocean. Before they could break camp the following morning, however, scouts returned with reports that the forest was impassible because of tangled underbrush and fallen logs. Smith and his party were forced to retrace their path to Trinity River. On May 28, Smith wrote in his journal:

I was obliged to ascend on to the range of hills and follow along their summits which was very difficult particularly as a dense fog rendered it almost impossible to select the best route. I encamped where there was very little grass and near where the Mountain made a rapid descent to the north rough and ragged with rocks. I went to the brink of the hill and when the fog cleared away for a moment I could see the country to the north extremely mountainous...From all appearances I came to the conclusion that I must move in again towards the coast.

Although the distance to the sea was only a few miles, Smith and his party required nearly 10 days to attain their goal. They were plagued with fog and rain that turned pathways to quagmires and hillsides to sheets of flowing mud. Many horses and mules died along the trail from lack of food. Near the coast, terrain became so rugged that Smith ordered his men to construct a rude pen for the horses, *"to keep them from rolling off."*

Historians who have studied journals of Smith's travels believe that he entered lands of Redwood National Park near

False Klamath Cove. On June 8, they established a camp in a grassy meadow near the sea and bartered with a family of Yurok Indians for mussels, clams and dried fish. Smith found the natives shrewd traders, however, for they divided their goods repeatedly to obtain maximum profits. On June 9, Smith killed three Roosevelt elk, bringing relief to the starving men. *The moody silence of hunger* (changed) *to the busy bustle of preparation for cooking and feasting. Men could be seen in every part of the camp with raw meat and half roasted in their hands devouring it with the greatest alacrity while from their preparations and remarks you would suppose that nothing less than 24 hours constant eating would satisfy their appetites.*

From their camp at False Klamath Cove, Smith and his men traveled north. They quickly found themselves once again in dense, coast redwood forest. After a night spent near Damnation Creek, they camped near headwaters of Nickel Creek and descended the following day to the beachshore near present-day Crescent City. For several days, the party rested.

Passing from the area of Redwood National Park, Jedediah Smith entered Oregon Territory on June 23. As they rode up the coast, the party advanced along the shore where possible but were frequently forced to make long detours. On July 14, as men cooked breakfast near Umpqua River, more than 100 Indians attacked the party. Seventeen of the twenty men were killed, leaving Jedediah Smith, Arthur Black and John Turner. Turner fought off and killed four natives before fleeing to warn Smith, who had been scouting a short distance from camp. They were quickly joined by Black, who was pulled down by three natives before escaping. The three men spent several weeks wandering through mountains with little to eat before reaching Fort Vancouver, an outpost of Hudson's Bay Company. During expeditions which followed, Smith was able to recover some of the furs stolen by his attackers. He died during an Indian attack on May 27, 1931 while traveling from Cimarron River to Santa Fe.

Warned that American trappers were encroaching on their territory by accounts of Smith's journey, agents of Hudson's Bay Company sent parties to California in 1828, led by Alexander R. McCloud and Peter S. Ogden. Both traveled inland, however, and did not enter lands of Redwood National Park. In 1831 a party of Americans led by Ewing Young, traveled north from Fort Ross to Eel River. Rather than follow the stream to its mouth, they turned east and eventually reached Sacramento Valley. **Josiah Gregg.** In 1848, Major Pierson B. Redding discovered gold while prospecting gravel bars of Trinity River, a few miles east of the park. Thousands of opportunists flocked from Sacramento Valley to the strike, and ships laden with miners flooded Trinidad Bay. One of those drawn to northcoast California was Dr. Josiah Gregg, a scientist, traveler and author.

In November, 1849, Gregg led a party of seven men from the Trinity gold fields toward the coast. Because Hupa Indians living near the mining camps led him to believe the trip was a short, eight-day ride, he and his men carried only enough rations for 10 days. They quickly found their path blocked by huckleberry, salmonberry and fallen trees. More than four weeks passed before they entered lands of Redwood National Park near Redwood Creek.

Researchers believe that Gregg's party may have followed an Indian trail from Bald Hills to Tall Trees Grove on Redwood Creek, then turned downstream until they reached Elk Prairie. Gregg describes in his journal magnificent redwood trees, some more than 22 feet *(6.7 m)* in diameter and more than 300 feet *(91 m)* tall. He eventually found his way to Trinidad, passing southward out of the park. Gregg did not reach civilization, however, for he died a short distance from Clear Lake, more than 150 miles *(241 km)* to the south. Survivors of his group made their way to San Francisco, where stories of their travels excited interest in the area.

Settlement and Mining. Guided by descriptions of Gregg's journey, shiploads of miners soon descended on Trinidad Bay from San Francisco. They followed the overland trail through Tall Trees Grove to gold fields on Trinity River and quickly spread to other streams. Other vessels rediscovered the mouth of Klamath River and established the boom-town settlement of Klamath City. Residents of the new community soon found the river bar treacherous to shipping and moved on. A few miles to the north, reports of gold on Smith River were fol-

lowed in 1853 by settlers that laid out Crescent City. Unlike the town of Klamath, the new city thrived to become a center for the miners. To the south, Humboldt Bay also attracted settlers. Towns quickly grew and prospered at Humboldt, Uniontown and Eureka.

In April, 1850, gold was discovered in the sands of Gold Bluff beach by J. K. Johnson of Trinidad. He gathered a few samples of the mineral, then hurried to Trinidad to obtain provisions. Upon his return, he discovered that changing tides had swept the gold away and gave up in disgust. In years that

LAGOON & MINING FLUMES ON GOLD BLUFF.

followed, several other miners stumbled upon, then lost, the shoreline gold of Redwood National Park.

In December, 1850, the first serious attempt was made to mine the sands of Gold Bluff beach. Businessmen of the Pacific Mining Company chartered a schooner filled with miners and sailed for shores near Trinidad Bay. Upon arrival at the beach, however, they found that its gold only appeared at certain times. Gold Bluff beach in 1850 was not the wide, sandy expanse seen by park visitors today. During periods of storm, ocean waves beat against the bluffs and washed quartz sand containing gold from the beach. For much of the year, it remained hidden. Miners watched their chance, then rushed into the surf to load mules with sand. Once more upon shore, they would pan or wash the sand to extract its gold. Because of the fine nature of the mineral, however, little was obtained, and the company failed.

Other men attempted to mine the bluffs in later years, but no one was able to solve the problem of separating fine gold from the nearby sand. Ambitious prospectors even tried dredging the sea bottom off bluff shores, and in April, 1873, Gold Bluffs Undersea Mining Company brought a peculiar collection of pumps, dredges, machinery and men to park beaches. Although large quantities of sand, mud, muck and shells were pumped from beneath the sea, no gold was taken.

Unsuccessful attempts to mine the riches of Gold Bluff beach continued until nearly 1920. Buildup of sand on the beach by that year prevented waves from washing gold from the bluffs, and the fortune hunters finally dwindled.

For many years, mining continued on streams flowing within the park. Tributaries of Smith and Klamath rivers yielded large quantities of the precious yellow metal. In early days of the strikes, most mining was done by individuals equipped with gold pans and cradles, rocking devices suitable for separating rich sands and gravel. Only the discovery of hydraulic mining with large hoses of high-pressure water ended such individual attempts. By 1900, most mining was handled by large firms.

Indian Wars and Establishment of Klamath Reservation. In 1854, the death of a Crescent City resident at Indian hands touched off a series of wars which lasted for many years. A. French had accompanied several other men while hunting near Bald Hills, then returned alone to his home. He was last seen near the fishing camp of a Yurok Indian named Black Mow. Vigilantes quickly arrested, tried and hung Black Mow, along with two companions.

The following year, war broke out at Klamath River. Miners left their claims and clustered near major camps for protection. They held mass meetings, and in January, 1855, decided to disarm the natives. Many Indians quickly complied with the order, but a few, led by a group called the Red Caps, refused.

The miners attacked several innocent villages, burning houses and committing outrages on native women. When the Indians retaliated, six whites were killed and two injured. Only the arrival of a cavalry detachment from Fort Humboldt prevented further outbreaks of violence.

On November 16, 1855, an Executive Order by President Franklin Pierce created Klamath River Indian Reservation, a strip of land extending 20 miles (32 km) upstream from the mouth of Klamath River. In September, 1857, a company of United States Army troops were moved to the area from Fort Jones in Siskiyou County. In a flat near present-day Klamath Glen, they established Fort Ter-Waw.

Outbreak of the Civil War in 1860 compelled the United States Army to recall the company, and in 1862, a volunteer detachment replaced men of the Fourth Infantry. For several months, conditions were good, but a sudden downpour of rain during the winter of 1860 caused Klamath River to rise and flood the outpost. By end of winter, only three buildings remained standing, and the post was abandoned in June, 1862.

Visitors to Redwood National Park may easily explore many areas of historical interest dating to the period of overland exploration and settlement. Areas visited by Jedediah Smith and Josiah Gregg are among the most scenic in the park. Smith camped for a time near False Klamath Cove, site of Lagoon Creek Fishing Access and ending point of the Coastal Trail from Requa. Visitors to Tall Trees Grove, located approximately seven miles (11.3 km) south of the Orick gateway, may view a crossing point used both by Gregg's party and miners who followed.

At the community of Klamath Glen, located 3.1 miles (5 km) east from U.S. Highway 101 along the north bank of Klamath River, stands the site of Fort Ter-Waw. Only a California State Historical Marker is visible, however, for Klamath River Indian Reservation was opened to settlers in April, 1894, and devastating floods and construction in the intervening years have destroyed any trace of the outpost. To the south, Gold Bluff beach offers visitors the opportunity to see a site of early mining. Like Fort Ter-Waw, little remains from early days, but near the north end of the beach, a few remnants of mining camp will be of interest.

DEVELOPMENT, LUMBERING AND PRESERVATION

The period beginning with discovery of gold on Trinity River in 1848 marks a time of change for lands of Redwood National Park. Trails and roads were carved from the wilderness to link major seaports such as Crescent City, Trinidad and Humboldt Bay with the gold fields. Within a few years, the need for overland supply drove roads first to Oregon from Crescent City, then south to San Francisco from Humboldt Bay. It was not until 1894 that the two communities were linked by a narrow, plank road, dusty in summer and muddy in winter. At the mouth of the Klamath, a ferry portaged cars across the wide river. Similar craft were used on Smith River at Catching's and Peacock's ferries.

Lumbering in the Redwoods. Even as settlers and miners descended on lands of the park, the first coast redwood were felled by lumbermen who realized the commercial potential of the big trees. The pioneer lumbermen were mostly easterners from Canada and Maine and were accustomed to smaller trees such as pine, spruce and fir. Despite lack of suitable equipment for handling the giant logs, first redwood lumber was shipped from Humboldt Bay in 1855. In a few years, thousands of board feet of timber made their way to ports around the world.

Ingenious methods were used in rendering coast redwood to lumber. In the forest, a tree was attacked by as many as 20 choppers. Because redwood broaden widely near the ground, the woodsmen carefully cut notches in the trunk as much as 20 feet (6.1 m) above ground. Into these notches went springboards, long narrow rails of iron-tipped wood which supported the weight of choppers who labored in massive undercuts. Such springboards often arced with the movement of the woodsmen, adding to the force of their swing.

Double-bladed axes used for falling coast redwood were massive tools, sometimes with handles six feet (1.8 m) or more in length. The tree finally fell to a prepared bed of boughs and underbrush in a broad, slow arc which allowed the men to scramble to safety. Such beds were necessary, for coast redwood is brittle and easily cracks and splits under impact.

After falling the tree, peelers quickly surrounded the trunk, stripping the thick, fibrous bark from its surface. Each tree was bucked into sections 10 *(3 m)* to 20 feet *(6.1 m)* long, then moved to the mill. When forestry first began in lands near Redwood National Park, coast redwood forests extended nearly from ridgetop to the sea. Lumbermen frequently logged the area surrounding their wharfs and mills first, then moved upslope. Streams and sloughs were filled with rafts of logs during low water in summer and fall. With coming of winter rains, massive jams of timber would flow downstream with rising waters to the mills. Those lumbermen with claims atop ravines built corduroy tramways of smaller trees for sliding cut trees to market. Horse, mule and oxen teams struggled under the watchful eyes of teamsters to move the logs downhill. In later years, they were replaced by steam donkeys which winched the logs downhill to waiting trains. Logs too large for either method of transport were frequently split by dynamite into more workable sections.

In early years, a wide variety of methods were used by mills to transform trees to lumber. At first, only small logs were cut, mostly by means of slash or circular saws. In remote sites where use of steam was impractical, even hand power was employed for a time. Men would position themselves above and below the log, grasping opposite ends of a vertical, crosscut-like saw. At a signal, the man below would pull the saw down, then wait for the upper to pull it back to its starting point. Such

backbreaking labor quickly died away as advancing technology provided gang and head-rig saws, capable of rendering even the largest timbers.

Even today, forestry remains an important industry in north-coast California. Visitors to lumber mills near the park may tour the manufacturing process involved in reducing coast redwood and other species to lumber for commercial sale.

Preservation of Coast Redwoods. Efforts to preserve the coast redwood forests of northern California date to the earliest days of settlement. In 1852, California legislator Henry A. Crabb introduced a bill proposing a redwood park, but it was ignored. A similar bill was proposed to United States Congress in 1879, when Secretary of the Interior Carl Schurtz recommended that two townships be withdrawn by the president for a coast redwood park. Like the earlier bill, it died in committee.

In 1902, the first successful attempt was made to preserve virgin coast redwood forest. Through the efforts of the Sempervirens Club of San Jose, the timbered region of Santa Cruz County, known today as Big Basin Redwoods State Park, was purchased. A few years later, in 1908, philanthropist William Kent donated Muir Woods to the federal government. President Theodore Roosevelt, through a proclamation, established the area as a National Monument.

Alarmed in 1918 by continued logging of many fine stands of coast redwood, John Merriam and many other influential citizens formed Save-The-Redwoods League. Throughout its more than 50 years, the league has purchased with donated funds, thousands of acres of redwoods that have been given to the State of California. In many cases, timberlands have been donated directly by benefactors which, together with purchased units, today form the core of the California State Park System. 160-acre *(64.7-hectare)* tract was located within what is now Prairie Creek Redwoods State Park. A short time later, stands of coast redwood now in Del Norte Coast Redwoods State Park were donated to the state by George F. Schwartz. In years that followed, major purchases and donations by the membership of Save-The-Redwoods League enlarged the two parks to their current boundaries. Jedediah Smith Redwoods State Park was similarly created following the 1929 donation of Frank D. Stout Grove to the State of California. Visitors to these state parks may see memorial markers depicting large donations of lands or money by individuals concerned with preservation of the redwoods.

In 1945, the most ambitious proposal for federal preservation of coast redwood forest was made by Congresswoman Helen

Gahagan Douglas of California. She advocated establishment of a national park to be called the Franklin Delano Roosevelt Memorial Redwood Forest, encompassing over 2,800,000 acres *(1,133,160 hectares)*. The boundaries proposed by Douglas included a coastal belt extending southward from Oregon nearly to Bodega Bay in Sonoma County. Despite heated arguments both for and against, no action was taken on the bill.

Establishment of Redwood National Park. In April, 1963, the National Geographic Society renewed interest in a national park to protect coast redwood forests. Aided by their donation of funds, the National Park Service undertook a special study of the region attempting to evaluate both protected lands and remaining areas suitable for preservation. Secretary of the Interior Stewart L. Udall submitted his recommendations to President Lyndon B. Johnson in autumn, 1964. He concluded that additional protection was necessary, that cutting was rapidly diminishing available lands, and suggested possible areas suitable for preservation.

The report sparked widespread controversy among foresters and conservationists throughout the country, as well as among governmental leaders and citizens living near proposed park lands. Opinions varied widely as to both size and location of the park. Leaders of Save-The-Redwoods League supported the proposal of the National Park Service but recommended a larger area which included complete watersheds. Experience of the league in Humboldt Redwoods State Park to the south had shown the folly of preserving lands downslope from private timber holdings. Members of the powerful Sierra Club pushed for a park much larger than the 53,600-acre *(21,691-hectare)* National Park Service proposal. Their plan called for a preserve of nearly 90,000 acres *(36,423 hectares)* which encompassed much of Redwood Creek watershed. The lumbermen, by comparison, suggested a park comprised mostly of already-protected lands found in existing redwood state parks. Several additional plans were proposed in months that followed.

On November 1, 1967, members of the Senate passed a bill calling for establishment of Redwood National Park. The lawmakers did not follow closely any existing plan, however. Instead, they described a compromise preserve of 64,000 acres

(25,901 hectares). After hearings both in northern California and Washington, D.C., the House of Representatives passed a similar bill fixing the park at 58,000 acres *(23,473 hectares)*. A joint conference committee resolved the differences between Senate and House versions on September 9, 1968 and announced a finalized park of 58,000 acres. They included federal lands in Mill, Prairie, Lost Man, Little Lost Man and Redwood creeks drainages, as well as nearly 40 miles *(64 km)* of scenic coastline. Three California State Parks were also authorized for inclusion: Prairie Creek Redwoods in Humboldt County, and Del Norte Coast and Jedediah Smith Redwoods in Del Norte County. President Lyndon B. Johnson signed the act on October 2, 1968. In November, his wife dedicated the preserve in a ceremony held near Bald Hills Road at Lady Bird Johnson Grove.

Following its establishment, Redwood National Park continued to arouse controversy. Conservationists felt that without additional acreage to round out complete watersheds, the park was incomplete. Timber industry spokesmen replied that plans for continual yield on private lands required the remaining acreage. The three state parks authorized for eventual inclusion within Redwood National Park remained in hands of the State of California. Only through continued efforts and planning shall such conflicts be resolved.

Visitors to the park who wish to explore the history of Redwood National Park during the era of lumbering and preservation may find many areas of interest. Near the junction of Mill Creek hiking trail and Howland Hill Road, visitors may walk upon a puncheon, or corduroy, road that once carried stagecoaches and mining wagons from Crescent City to Oregon Territory. Throughout both federal and state lands, many remnants of early forestry may be seen, including railway routes, stumps marked with springboard marks and artifacts such as old crosscut saws and cables. Dedication plaques marking the accomplishments of early conservationists and benefactors of Save-The-Redwoods League dot many scenic groves. On Bald Hills Road, a short walk allows visitors to see the dedication site at Lady Bird Johnson Grove. At this spot, the conservation and preservation efforts of thousands of individuals were recognized with establishment of Redwood National Park.

Redwood National Park is located in a geographic region which has been folded and faulted into rugged, erosionally-unstable mountain ranges with low to moderate relief. These mountains line the Pacific edge of northern California in a wide belt and are called the California Coast Range. Within the park, the California Coast Range is comprised of sharp ridgelines and trough-shaped valleys. Rivers and streams follow its valleys northwest to the Pacific Ocean.

The geologic features of Redwood National Park are very complex and puzzle even trained geologists. Because heavy vegetation and soil cover seldom allow close examination of bedrock, researchers must frequently rely on inconclusive evidence when constructing theories to explain features found within the park. Such theories rely, in great part, on recently-developed knowledge of worldwide concepts such as sea floor spreading and crustal plate tectonics. The relationship of these concepts to park geology is not perfectly understood, and revision may be necessary as research of Redwood National Park yields more complete understanding of the region.

GEOLOGIC HISTORY

Most geologists believe many rocks seen today by visitors to Redwood National Park began collecting as sediment in a deep, ocean trench during late Jurassic geologic times, nearly 140 million years ago. The location of seas at that time were greatly different from those of today, and researchers feel ocean may once have extended as far inland as present Utah and Wyoming. The ocean-floor trench paralleled closely present northern

California coastlines and linked continental and oceanic crust. River-transported silt and rocks were deposited on the ocean bottom for nearly 70 million years.

Mixing and deformation of trench rock sediments ended sea-floor deposition approximately 70 million years ago. Moving along great faultlines of weakness, rocks of the oceanic crust and mantle mixed with both sediments and continental crust to form a jumbled body known as the Franciscan Formation. This period of earth history is known by geologists as the Coast Range Orogeny. Within rocks of the Franciscan Formation, visitors may see ancient sandstone and pebble conglomerates mixed with volcanic rocks from deep within the crust.

The Coast Range Orogeny ended about 40 to 60 million years ago, during Eocene times. Scientists believe that movement along the San Andreas fault relieved pressures between the oceanic crust and the continental land mass. Frequent earthquakes continue today throughout the length of the San Andreas fault.

Oldest Rock. Oldest rocks in Redwood National Park are those of Kerr Ranch Schist. Most of the southern inland portion of the park is based upon such schist, and visitors may view many outcrops along Redwood Creek trail and stream. Kerr Ranch Schist is also exposed in roadcuts along U.S. Highway 101, south of the Orick gateway.

The age of Kerr Ranch Schist is not definitely known. Scientists believe it is older than rocks formed during the Coast Range Orogeny and may be more than 135 million years in age. Kerr Ranch Schist was originally comprised of mixed sedimentary and igneous, or molten, rocks. It has been strongly metamorphosed by long exposure to heat and pressure, and few traces of original rocks remain. Intrusions of basalt cut through Kerr Ranch Schist at many points. Such basalt is chemically similar to granite and formed when molten rock, or magma, was forced under great pressure into near-surface deposits to later cool. Such intrusions of basalt often have altered within the schist to greenstone, a gritty, jade-like rock.

Soils developed from rocks of Kerr Ranch Schist frequently contain oxidized iron that colors it earthy red. Visitors to the park may see such soil in roadcuts along U.S. Highway 101 approximately 2.8 miles *(4.5 km)* west of the Orick gateway.

Franciscan Formation. Next youngest among park rocks are those of Franciscan Formation, formed 70 to 140 million years ago. Visitors may best see rocks of Franciscan Formation in roadcuts while traveling U.S. Highway 101 north between Klamath River and Crescent City, but may also view such formation along Redwood Creek, about one mile *(1.6 km)* upstream from its confluence with Bridge Creek.

Franciscan rocks consist both of hardened marine sediments and igneous rocks from beneath the ocean floor. Some geologists believe rocks which originated as deeply in the earth as the mantle layer, today lie exposed in Franciscan Formation.

Because Franciscan rocks were long deformed by heat and pressure, metamorphic rocks are common. Such metamorphic rocks include volcanic greenstone, meta-sedimentary rocks, and very-altered eclogite. Only slightly deformed metamorphic rocks, however, are common in Redwood National Park. Visitors may occasionally view high-grade metamorphic blueschist pebbles along the stream bed of Redwood Creek. Such pebbles were carried downstream by the creek from its upper drainage, south of park boundaries.

Through the length of its exposure, Franciscan Formation is sheared by faults. At its boundary with Kerr Ranch Schist, for example, the formation is cut by Grogan fault. Franciscan rocks have been so-deformed by faults that they often consist of isolated blocks of various rock types, ranging in size from two feet *(.6 m)* to five miles *(8 km)*. Such blocks are called melange and are often bordered by fault-sheared, fine-grained powder called gouge.

Uplift and Erosion. The geologic history of Redwood National Park following the Coast Range Orogeny is mostly one of uplift and erosion. Following deposition and deformation of Franciscan Formation, fault action raised park lands above sea level. Erosion during Tertiary times, 12 to 70 million years ago, lowered most of the area to a wide plain with meandering rivers and few hills. No sedimentary rocks from that time are believed preserved in Redwood National Park, and visitors may instead view uplifted remnants of the erosional plain, visible as flat-topped ridges near the present seacoast. Ancient stream gravel is occasionally discovered to east, outside park boundaries and corresponds in age to erosion of Tertiary park rocks. These deposits commonly contain placer gold and were prospected by miners from 1850 to 1890. Such gold may once have originated in rock formations of Klamath Mountains, located east of the park.

Following erosion during Tertiary times, changing sea levels again covered Redwood National Park. Miocene marine sediments nearly 12 million years old may be seen by park visitors near Crescent City gateway. Flat, wave-cut terraces of that time are uplifted today more than 2200 feet *(671 m)* above sea level and include patches of thin, deeply weathered sediments known as the Wymer Beds. Such deposits contain many fossils and are best exposed approximately 12 miles *(19.3 km)* southeast of Crescent City.

Geologists who study the park frequently have difficulty separating Miocene deposits found within Redwood National Park from later Pliocene sediments. Where such mixed deposits occur, they are called Neogene, or 2 to 25 million years, in age. Most Neogene rocks have been uplifted and eroded following deposition, and visitors to the park may best view them in seacliffs at Gold Bluff beach. They are also exposed in roadcuts along U.S. Highway 101 near Prairie Creek Redwoods State Park. Outside park boundaries, Neogene sediments may be seen as Saint George Formation, located 1.3 miles *(2.1 km)* northwest of the Crescent City gateway at Pebble Beach.

Park rocks of Neogene age often contain river deposits of sand and gravel, transported by Pliocene streams approximately five million years ago. Like sediments of earlier age found outside park boundaries, gold frequently accompanies such sand and gravel deposits. Several attempts were made to mine gold at Gold Bluff beach during the last century but were abandoned around 1900. Prospectors found such gold too fine-grained for economical separation.

Hardened Neogene sediments include siltstones, sandstones and pebbly conglomerates. Geologists have found fossil wood and leaves of ancient trees within such rock, and northwest of Crescent City at Pebble Beach, such fossils are common. They occur as part of Saint George Formation and are two to seven million years old.

Less than two million years ago, the growth and melting of glacial ice which affected much of the northern hemisphere combined with continued uplift of park lands to produce great fluctuations in sea level. Although glaciers did not reach Redwood National Park, visitors may view within its boundaries the effect of such ice advances upon the sea. Wave-cut benches, or terraces, are common features of park seacoasts. Such ancient terraces formed during periods of wave erosion and are similar, in many respects, to those currently developing beneath offshore waters.

Ancient marine terraces may best be viewed near the Crescent City gateway, where coastal flats formed between last advances of glacial ice. Several other terrace features may be seen south of Redwood National Park at Patrick's Point State Park, and near the community of Trinidad.

Sea terraces found within the park are often capped by deposits of loosely-packed sand. Examples of such capping deposits include sediments of Battery Formation, visible to park visitors at Crescent City. Battery Formation sands are believed to be less than 10,000 years in age. In some places near Crescent City, such sediment caps older exposures of Saint George Formation.

Metamorphic Deformation. Geologists have identified two trends regarding metamorphic alteration of deposits formed less than 40 million years ago. Such deformation seems generally less intense north than south, and older sediments seem more deformed than recent sediments. These trends suggest to geologists that deformation of rocks within Redwood National Park is a continuing process which most affects sediments near the southern boundary.

Visitors to the park may observe the effect of metamorphic trends shaping rock of the redwood region while approaching the Orick gateway from the south. Miocene deposits found south of the park, near Eel River, are strongly folded and may include overthrust Cretaceous rocks. At the southern boundary, more recent Pliocene rocks near Prairie Creek Redwoods State Park have been tilted by fault uplift, yet remain only slightly affected. Recent Pleistocene deposits nearest Crescent City appear least deformed.

RECENT GEOLOGIC FEATURES

Fault uplift of Redwood National Park continues today. Frequent, mild earthquakes result in measurable, yearly changes which increase the relief of park mountains. As result of such uplift, many deposits and geologic features are exposed within rocks of Kerr Ranch Schist, over 135 million years old. A short distance to the west lie sediments of the Franciscan Formation, 70 to 140 million years in age. Ancient marine terraces step downward in elevation and age toward present sea level, while nearest the sea are most recent deposits.

Geologic processes also continue to shape park lands. Among the features formed within Redwood National Park since retreat of the last Pleistocene glaciers, visitors may view lagoons, floodplains, river terraces, beaches, landslides and earthflows.

Lagoons. Seaside lagoons common to the southern portion of Redwood National Park were formed following rises in sea level less than 5000 years ago. Such sea level fluctuations have drowned the former ocean mouths of many park streams to form bays, lagoons and marshy, level river valleys. Lower Redwood Creek valley, upon which the community of Orick has been built, was once such a seacoast bay. River transported sediment has completely filled its former mouth.

Wave action may build sand bars, or longshore spits, across less active streams and form lagoons. Such spits are porous, and generally allow excess river water to pass through them to the sea. During periods of heavy precipitation and high runoff, however, lagoons may breach their spits in wide openings called mouths.

Visitors to Redwood National Park may easily see seaside lagoons near the southwest boundary. Freshwater Lagoon is the largest water body located within the park. It is situated two miles *(3.2 km)* southwest of the Orick gateway on U.S. Highway 101, which divides lagoon waters from the Pacific Ocean. A concrete overflow located near the northwest end of the lagoon prevents interruption of highway traffic during periods of high water. Freshwater Lagoon is so named because it contains little salt. Outside park boundaries, a few miles to

south, visitors may explore both Stone and Big Lagoon, which are part of Dry Lagoon State Park. Both lagoons contain briny, undrinkable water.

Floodplains and River Terraces. River floodplains may often extend up park streams for many miles. Such plains form during periods of heavy precipitation when rivers overflow their banks to deposit silt, sand and gravel. Because steep slopes are common to river valleys of the California Coast Range, many floodplains are broken into small, interrupted segments. As river waters erode downward through underlying rock, canyons form and leave small portions of floodplain stranded above current seasonal deposition. Such remnant floodplains are known as river terraces.

Visitors to Redwood Creek trail may best view both river floodplains and terraces at Tall Trees Grove, about seven miles *(11.3 km)* southeast of the Orick gateway. Upstream from Tall Trees Grove, ancient river terraces may rise 100 *(30.5 m)* to 200 feet *(61 m)* above present stream level. Such terraces probably were formed by ancient Pleistocene rivers, nearly 10,000 years ago. Visitors may also view river floodplains near Requa, where Klamath River joins the Pacific Ocean in a wide valley. Deposition of sediment on Klamath floodplain occurs almost yearly.

Beaches. Visitors may easily visit beaches and seacliffs common to the park seacoast. Beaches found within Redwood National Park have greatly widened during recent years. Researchers who study the park believe that such beach widening may result from large quantities of sediment introduced by the forestry and mining activities of man. When gold was discovered at Gold Bluff beach in 1850, waves often washed the base of its seacliffs. Today, even storm waves seldom reach Gold Bluffs.

Hydraulic mining may yield abundant sand and silt which is carried downriver to the sea. Erosion of hillsides following cutting of nearby timber may also provide sources for increased sediment. Rivers and streams of northcoast California erode and transport more sediment per acre of drainage area than any comparable water system in the United States. Redwood Creek, for example, may carry over 16 tons *(14,515 kg)* of sediment per acre *(.4 hectare)* of basin each year.

Beaches 1.8 miles *(2.9 km)* south of the Crescent City gate-way also provide visitors with the opportunity to examine sand dunes. Dune deposits cap many park marine terraces with sand. Such sand dunes consist of an active growth area where wind-transported sand from the sea is deposited in crescent-shaped bodies which move slowly inland. Dunes are often sculptured by wind-formed ripple marks. Further inland, vegetative growth eventually stops dune movement. Small remnant dunes may also be seen by visitors to Big Lagoon, 4.8 miles *(7.7 km)* south of Redwood National Park on U.S. Highway 101.

Landslides and Earthflows. The forces of erosion are very ac-tive in Redwood National Park. Such activity may often result in landslides and earthflows which affect widespread areas. The sheared and fractured nature of park rock combines with per-iods of high, concentrated rainfall to rapidly weather nearby slopes and hillsides.

Landslides are the most common erosional process of the park. Such slides may move dirt, rock and vegetation downslope into streams. Moved material, or detritus, is then eroded by river waters and carried downstream to river floodplains and the sea. Landslides involving large areas have occasionally blocked Redwood Creek with temporary dams.

Within the park, large, slow-moving landslides called earth-flows frequently occur. Such flows have shaped much of the park landscape. Earthflows may be seen by visitors as scars along U.S. Highway 101, north of the Orick gateway. Earth-flows are also common east of Redwood Creek, where prairies extend from Bald Hills road nearly to the stream.

Because the land of Redwood National Park is naturally unstable, disturbance of its slopes and streams may greatly accelerate erosion. Such disturbance may result either from natural events, or from the activities of man. Erosion rates during the past 25 years in Redwood Creek drainage have greatly increased. Researchers who study the stream attribute such erosion both to foresting of river slopes, and to natural causes which include severe floods in 1955 and 1964.

Mild, wet winters and cool summers with frequent coastal fog best describe weather conditions found within Redwood National Park. Best opportunities for good weather occur during late spring and early autumn, when skies are generally blue and sunny with comfortably warm temperatures. Fortunately, however, there is much variation, and visitors should come prepared for warm and sunny, as well as cool and moist weather.

Climate. The climates of northern California and southwestern Oregon rely in great part on weather systems originating in mid-ocean waters of the north Pacific. A marine high pressure area controls moisture-laden air flowing throughout most of the year to western North America. In summer, this marine high pressure system shifts northward and forces storm tracts eastward into British Columbia and southeastern Alaska. Visitors to the park during summer may expect long periods of northwesterly winds with little rainfall.

With coming of winter, the system of high pressure air moves slowly southward, allowing storms to approach the coast from southwest. Passing over warm waters of the Pacific, such storms commonly become laden with moisture and bring abundant rain and southerly winds to Redwood National Park.

Other effects on climate result from changes in position of the Pacific high pressure system. Moist air flowing from the northwest during summer moves ocean waters of the California Current, causes upwelling of deep-sea water near the coast, and layers the shore with blankets of fog. The California Current originates near Japan and is commonly several degrees warmer than surrounding ocean water to east or west. It flows southward along the coast nearly to the equator before merging with waters of the East Pacific Drift. Near the coast of Redwood National Park, the current passes an area of upwelling, where winds from the mid-Pacific high circulate cold water from deep within the ocean to the surface in a belt 25 *(40 km)* to 50 miles *(80 km)* wide. Warmed and moistened by the waters of the offshore California Current, then suddenly cooled by near-shore upwelling water, the wind condenses in dense banks of coastal fog. Such fog is swept inland by the northwest summer winds and blankets the coast during evening and morning hours. Midday heat from inland regions of the park may lift and break coastal fog into low clouds which quickly evaporate.

Rainfall. Most rainfall in Redwood National Park occurs between the months of October and April. The park commonly receives 60 to 100 days of measurable rainfall each year, mostly during storms lasting two to five days. A typical winter storm in Redwood National Park is comprised of intermittent rain for three days, followed by 7 to 14 days of overcast with little rain. Occasionally, the park may experience heavy, persistant rains lasting 7 to 10 days. Such rains may bring widespread flooding along river floodplains.

The heaviest recorded historical rainfall in California occurred near boundaries of the park in 1909, when Monumental Station received 153.4 inches *(390 cm)* of annual precipitation. Monumental Station is located in Del Norte County, at an elevation of 2750 feet *(838 m)*.

Average annual precipitation within Redwood National Park ranges between 70 *(178 cm)* and 72 inches *(183 cm)* per year. Such precipitation most commonly occurs as rainfall, although occasional hail and snow may fall atop park ridges. Heavy rainfall is believed by researchers of the park to be a primary reason for the restriction of coast redwood growth to northern California and southwestern Oregon.

Temperature. Redwood National Park seldom experiences extreme heat or cold. Near the park, for example, the January mean temperature is 47 degrees F *(8.3 C)* while August is just 57 degrees F *(13.9 C)*. Visitors to the park may expect broader temperature ranges with increasing distance from the coast. Such temperature variation results in great part from cooling

and warming of the air mass by Pacific Ocean waters. The ocean cools the lands of Redwood National Park during summer and warms it in winter.

The mean annual temperature for Klamath, located near the center of Redwood National Park, is 52.8 degrees F *(11.6 C)*. Rarely, temperatures may range as high as 100 degrees F *(37.8 C)* or as low as 15 degrees F *(-9.4 C)*.

Microclimates. Much vegetation seen by visitors to Redwood National Park grows as a result of favorable climatic conditions peculiar to coast redwood forest. Known as microclimates, such favorable conditions result from both shade and moisture retention qualities of the forest. Beneath groves of mature redwood, visitors may notice the chilly quality of the air or may occasionally require a sweater even on warmest summer days. Temperature beneath such trees may be 15 degrees F *(8.3 C)* lower than comparable meadow areas nearby. Shading also reduces soil moisture evaporation, permitting growth of ferns, mosses and fungi. Visitors to the park may explore the microclimates of coast redwood forest near visitor campgrounds or by walking many hiking trails.

THE COAST REDWOODS

Visitors to Redwood National Park may explore among its virgin redwood groves the beauty of wilderness forest. Known worldwide for their size and grandeur, coast redwood grow naturally only in coastal California and the extreme southwest corner of Oregon. Such trees are generally believed tallest among living plants. Their forests are cathedral-like, and few fail to be awed when standing beneath the crowns of these forest giants.

Included among coast redwood of the park are the Howard A. Libby and Frank D. Stout trees. Located on an alluvial bench of flood-washed silt near Redwood Creek, the Howard A. Libby, or Tall Tree rises 367.8 feet *(112.1 m)* from its base near Redwood Creek. The Libby tree is tallest among coast redwood. The Stout Tree may be seen by visitors to Jedediah Smith Redwoods State Park. While not as tall a tree, at 340 feet *(103.6 m)* Stout Tree contains the largest bulk of known coast redwoods and is over 20 feet *(6.1 m)* diameter at chest height.

Other claims are common regarding coast redwood. They are not largest of living things; the Stout Tree is dwarfed by Sierra big tree redwoods, many of them 250 *(76.2 m)* to 300 feet *(91.4 m)* in height and between 20 *(6.1 m)* and 30 feet *(9.1 m)* in diameter. Largest of big tree redwood is General Sherman Tree in Sequoia-Kings Canyon National Park. The Sherman tree is only 272 feet *(82.9 m)* tall, but is 27.5 feet *(8.4 m)* in diameter, six feet *(1.8 m)* above the ground. The tree may weigh as much as 6167 tons *(5,594,579 kg)*.

Nor is coast redwood the oldest living thing; both big tree redwood and bristlecone pine are older. Recent claims for oldest tree include giant Formosan sun trees of Taiwan, thought to be more than 6000 years old. Even such trees, however, are dwarfed in age by a simple woody shrub, the box huckleberry of Virginia. Box huckleberry, which may form colonies miles wide, is over 13,000 years of age, almost 11,000 years greater than known coast redwood.

Prehistory. For 2000 years, Native Americans have lived on fringes of coast redwood forests now found within Redwood National Park. The Yuroks built dugout canoes and plank dwellings of redwood, mostly from fallen or flood-transported trees found on nearby major streams and rivers. Although Natives sometimes used fire to fall trees, cutting mature redwood without iron tools was beyond their means.

Indians residing near the park recount the following legend regarding origin of the coast redwood:

In the beginning, the great spirit Wah-Peck-oo-May-ow populated the world with trees, mountains, people, rivers and all the things that came to be. Redwood trees were made to be great warriors. Some were taller, straighter, of better color, with branches that began higher from the ground. Such trees were the best of warriors.

To protect the redwood, Wah-Peck-oo-May-ow gathered barks of the Cascara, the dogwood, the fern, and other bitter herbs. He first dried them in the sun, then ground them to powder and mixed them with swamp water. Then the great spirit poured his medicine over the boughs and trunks of the redwood tree. His magic made its wood so bitter that fire would not eat it. To this day, redwood does not burn easily.

After the great spirit had made the birds, the mountains and the redwood trees, he climbed a very high mountain which was always covered with snow, even in heat of summer. From this mountain, he could speak clearly to all gathered on the earth below. He decreed that redwood must not be used for firewood and that humans could only build their homes and canoes from it.

Then Wah-Peck-oo-May-ow urged all Indians to show great respect to their redwood warriors. In time, Indian men would shoot an arrow high into the air, aiming at spots in certain tall, straight redwood trees just below the first limbs. This gesture was a sign of admiration, recognition and salute.

Indian women with boy babies would remove the children from their carrier basket, then hold them high facing the warrior tree. If the baby laughed, they believed it would grow tall and straight like the tree to be a brave warrior. Young women without children would sing softly a love song of admiration to the warrior redwoods.

Discovery of the Coast Redwood. First men to look upon coast redwood were probably decendents of ice-age explorers who crossed a narrow land bridge separating Asia and North America nearly 10,000 years ago. These nomadic hunters, fishermen and gatherers were ancesters of Native Americans of today.

In 458 A.D., first non-native man may have viewed coast redwoods. In explorations of that year, Chinese epic explorer Hui Shan noted tall trees with red wood while sailing the Pacific rim near what may have been the coast of California. His writings form records recently rediscovered by Chinese historians. Such records have prompted controversy regarding discovery of North America.

First European explorer to view coast redwood was probably Captain Juan Rodriquez Cabrillo, who in 1542 named the region of Alta California off which he sailed, "the coast of pines." He did not land, however, and no evidence exists that he felt the tall, stately trees unique.

Sir Francis Drake and Sebastian Cermeno likewise failed to mention coast redwood in their journals written during travels of California coastlines.

The historical figure normally credited with discovery of coast redwood is Don Gaspar de Portola, who led an exploratory party into central California in 1769. On October 10, Fray Juan Crespi noted in his diary that the Portola expedition marched into an area of low hills. It was forested heavily with very tall trees of unusual color. He wrote, "although the wood resembles cedar somewhat in color, it is very different." Miguel Costanso recorded that one tree was "the largest, highest and straightest tree" he and his comrades had ever seen. The party named them *palo colorado* (red tree) for their unusual color.

Forty years after Portola's explorations, coast redwood were recognized by botanists as a unique species. In a collection dated 1794, Archibald Menzies, a surgeon and botanist of the George Vancouver expedition of 1792-1793, included for the first time, examples of coast redwood foliage.

Addition of scientific names for genus and species of coast redwood was made in 1847, when noted Hungarian botanist Stephen Endlicher named the tree *Sequoia sempervirens.* Endlicher did not specify his source, but it is commonly believed that his name for genus honors a Cherokee Indian named Sequoyah. Also known by his Christian name, George Gist, Sequoyah never visited the redwood region, and is instead best remembered for his one-man development of an 83-character alphabet of the Cherokee language. His alphabet is based on syllables, and is similar in many respects to Kata Kana, the written alphabet of modern Japanese. Sequoyah's name means "oppossum" in his native Cherokee tongue.

Endlicher's species name, *sempervirens,* has been variously translated as meaning "evergreen," or "everlasting." Evidence indicates that Endlicher intended the former, botanical meaning.

NATURAL HISTORY OF THE COAST REDWOOD

Forests of the Past. Redwood which visitors view in the park groves today represent only minute fractions of once-huge forests of ancient times. The oldest fossil evidence of early redwood is thought to be a preserved foliage specimen dating to Jurassic geologic times, 175 million years ago. *Taxodiaceae,* the family of plants to which coast redwood belong, is much older. The group first became distinct during the Triassic period of the Mesozoic era, 200-300 million years ago.

By 130 million years ago, ancestors of coast redwood had spread widely throughout the world. Tall trees similar to those seen today in Redwood National Park were found growing in North America, Greenland, Iceland, Europe, and central and east Asia. Cause of the success of redwood during Cretaceous times lies primarily in the widespread moist climate extensive during that period. Abundant moisture and warmth promoted huge growths of plant and treè life, often extending further north than is common today. Such ancient plantlife is termed

Arcto-Tertiary Geoflora by scientists, because it reached the peak of its northward expansion during early Tertiary times, 70 million years ago.

Forest trees of Arcto-Tertiary Geoflora included both conifer evergreens and deciduous, or leaf-losing, trees. Among the conifers, redwood were abundant, and ancestors of tall trees of today extended as far north as Ellesmere Island, above the present Arctic Circle.

Evolution of the Coast Redwood. Many scientists today believe coast redwood evolved as result of cross-fertilization between metasequoia, or dawn, redwood and some now-extinct tree resembling Sierra big tree redwood, taiwania, or Tasmanian cedar. The species probably spread via land bridges from a restricted region of west-central North America to widespread areas around the world.

For millions of years, coast redwood flourished. Moist fog and mild temperatures nutured the tall trees while abundant rainfall aided their growth. Climatic conditions remained unchanged for millions of years. Only with Eocene times, 58 million years ago, did redwood forests begin retreat. Moist, humid areas shrank, and forests of trees withdrew before masses of cool, dry, glacial air. In Europe, coast redwood abandoned Scandanavia, Germany and Spain. Stopped in their flight by waters of the Mediterranean Sea, they became extinct. Vast areas of Asia and North America lost, in turn, their redwood forests to southward-spreading shields of glacial ice.

By end of the Ice Age, only scattered fragments of once-worldwide coast redwood forests remained. Today, the natural range of redwood extends southward from two groves on Chetco River in extreme southwestern Oregon, to Salmon Creek Canyon in southern Monterey County, California. They are confined to an irregular, narrow coastal strip about 450 miles *(724 km)* long and five *(8 km)* to 35 miles *(56 km)* wide.

Habitat. Coast redwood live today in a region which has been geologically folded and faulted into great northwestward-trending trenches and ridges. Major streams and rivers of northern California follow these folds through mountains of the Coast Range. Lands of the north coast are unstable, and wide-

spread erosion and landsliding are common. In spite of rugged terrain, total relief for a mountainous region is small. Only occasionally do peaks rise above 4000 feet *(1219 m)*. Highest point within Redwood National Park is Holter Ridge, 2260 feet *(689 m)*, located approximately six miles *(9.6 km)* southwest of Prairie Creek Redwoods State Park. Within the park, redwood grow from sea level to ridgetop. Best stands have developed on riverside flats along Smith River to the north and near Redwood Creek in the south. Climate within the park is generally mild, and mean annual temperatures remain near 60 degrees F *(15.6 C)* throughout most of the year. Only rarely do temperatures fall below 15 degrees F *(-9.4 C)* or climb above 100 degrees F *(37.8 C)*.

Annual precipitation may vary from 25 inches *(63.5 cm)* in exceptionally dry years to 122 inches *(310 cm)* during extremely wet ones. Most precipitation occurs as winter rain, although occasional snow, sleet and hail may occur. Frequent summer fogs promote moist conditions favorable to coast redwood growth. Some researchers believe such coastal fog is of greater importance to redwood growth than actual precipitation. Humid fogs tend to decrease water loss from evaporative transpiration. Such fog may also add moisture to forest soils and ground cover.

Coast redwood growing near the sea often may not tolerate direct ocean winds well. Researchers who study coast redwood growth feel that sea wind sensitivity may be due to low windborn-salt tolerance. Such salt frequently distorts young redwood trees growing near the sea. Coast redwood sometimes grow in protective lees of other species, particularly Sitka spruce and Douglas fir. Where such growth occurs, redwood may be found close to the water edge.

Near ridgetops, where both dryness and steepness of slope increases, redwood trees are often smaller. In such areas, winter snows and prevailing winds make less hospitable conditions common, and Douglas fir and tanoak may replace coast redwood with rapid transitions from lowland forest. Visitors to Redwood National Park may notice such succession of forest species while traveling routes where elevation and distance from the ocean increases.

COAST REDWOOD GROWTH

Coast redwood found within Redwood National Park are among fastest growing of trees. They reach greater heights than any other living thing. In favorable growth conditions, trees 20 years old may average 51 feet *(15.5 m)* in height and eight inches *(20.3 cm)* in diameter. Average mature trees soar from 200 *(61 m)* to 240 feet *(73.2 m)* tall with diameters of 10 *(3 m)* to 15 feet *(4.6 m)*. Exceptional individuals may sometimes reach heights greater than 350 feet *(106.7 m)*, diameters of nearly 20 feet *(6.1 m)* and ages as great as 2200 years. Forces of chance which affect coast redwood include fire, aridity, infertility, frost, and competing plantlife.

Flowering and Fruiting. Coast redwood begin life as blooms which form on mature parent trees between late November and early March. Both male and female flowers may be found, although such are seldom seen by visitors due to height above the forest floor and small size. The tiny male flowers release clouds of sulphur-colored pollen which are carried on forest winds to waiting female buds.

Weather conditions during pollination may affect redwood seed development. If flowers open during continuous rainy periods, pollen may wash from male flowers, or strobili, and may not pollinate female conelets. In such cases, little, if any fertilization of ovules occurs. Best dispersal of pollen occurs when prolonged dry spells make easy its release from male buds.

About five months after fertilization of ovules, or conelets, redwood cones become mature. Redwood cones are usually ovular in shape and about .5 *(1.3 cm)* to 1.2 inches *(3 cm)* long. Such tiny cones release their seed while still on the tree. Cones may remain empty on trees long after all seeds are gone but finally fall to the forest floor.

Seed Production. Mature coast redwood produce cones and seed nearly every year. Many redwood begin regular cone and seed development at 20 years of age. Some researchers believe that optimum cone and seed production occurs between 20 and 250 years of age. Many exceptions, however, have been found by foresters who study redwood. Trees over 500 years may bear abundant cones, but little seed is viable. The Howard A. Libby Tree, tallest in the world, is believed to be more than 400 years old. Its cones and seed recently have been collected for experiments attempting to develop faster growing species of redwood for commercial use. Cones of coast redwood have few natural enemies. Western gray squirrel, chickaree, and Townsend chipmunks may gather such cones while foraging. Occasional damage is caused by insect pests, including larvae known as roundheaded borer. Only fire may cause widespread cone failure. Coast redwood which have been damaged by fire commonly cease cone and seed production for four to five years following injury. Even such trees, however, recover eventually and renew reproduction activity.

Redwood cones have 15 to 20 scales, each scale normally producing two to five seeds. Such seeds are minute in size, and 120,000 may weigh less than one pound (.45 kilo). Redwood seed often averages less than 10 per cent viability. Such poor average germination often is caused by high percentages of empty or tannin-filled seed, rather than by dormancy. When obviously empty seed are removed, germination success may reach 79 per cent.

Seed Dissemination. Completion of seed dispersal from mature coast redwood cones may require several months. Redwood cones dry readily when weather conditions are favorable, but the mature period from mid-September through late March is seldom without rain or moist fog. Abundant precipitation may serve to slow seed release by delaying cone opening, or speed it by dissolving tannic acid crystals commonly found within cones. Altitude and wind exposure may also commonly affect seed release.

Despite small size, redwood seed falls rapidly when released. Such seed lacks efficient wings often found on other species and may remain less than 400 feet (122 m) from its parent tree.

Vegetative Reproduction. In addition to growth from seed, coast redwood commonly develop from sprouts on injured or fallen trees. Even windblown branches may develop root systems under ideal conditions. Few other conifers match this ability to sprout, often within three weeks of damage to parent trees. Sprouting in redwood most commonly occurs when parent root systems are either wholly or partially undamaged following loss of trunk and crown. At such times, numerous, vigorous sprouts may develop from dormant buds which circle the root collar and broken trunk. Sprouts utilize the developed root systems of parent trees to compete with neighboring trees for sunlight, moisture and soil nutrients. Researchers believe sprouts which develop along sides of stumps or snags may be weaker than those from root collars.

While any coast redwood may sprout abundantly, vegetative reproduction is often better on good forest sites. Researchers believe such reproductive capability decreases with both age and size of parent trees.

Under ideal conditions, sprouts may form along the entire length of both fallen and standing trees. Trees which have been fire damaged, mechanically injured, or which grow on sites suddenly flooded with abundant sunlight, may also form numerous sprouts, even when original crown foliage remains. Such trees develop many branches and dense foliage and have been called "fire-columns" by foresters. New and larger crowns may develop from sprout growth unless injuries have so weakened the tree as to cause death.

Burls. Coast redwood commonly develop masses of growth buds similar to those which produce vegetative sprouts. Such clusters are called burls, and may occasionally reach weights of 500 pounds *(227 kg)*. Burls frequently form on trees which have been injured but may also develop on young trees.

At approximately six months of age, most redwood seedlings have a tiny burl at each root collar. Collar burls normally remain dormant until fire damage or other injury occurs. At such times, burls may develop hardy shoots which guarantee survival of the seedling.

Small burls are commonly collected for commercial sale by souvenir dealers near Redwood National Park. Visitors may stimulate growth in souvenir burls by placing them in a shallow pan of water. Such burls then develop feathery sprouts which make attractive centerpieces. Sprout development may continue for several years, but lack of development hormone prevents formation of roots.

Seedling Establishment and Development. Coast redwood seed may germinate soon after falling from its cone. Moist mineral soil and mild weather are important to germination, however, and such growth usually occurs in March and April. Best development occurs when seeds are lightly covered by soil. Provided that moisture is adequate, seed may also, however, germinate readily in duff, on logs, in debris and under other vegetation. Redwood seed usually yields seedlings within three weeks. Such seedlings most frequently have two leaves, or cotyledons, on a stem usually less than one inch *(2.5 cm)* in height.

New redwood seedlings require greater supplies of soil moisture than most competing forest species. Adequate supplies of rain in spring and summer may, therefore, be critical to seedling survival. Because young redwood trees evaporate more water by transpiration than other species, long periods of relatively low humidity may serve to desicate and kill seedling foliage. Redwood seedlings also have no root hairs and are unable to efficiently extract soil moisture.

Best redwood growth occurs on sites where favorable water conditions result from high rainfall, humid air, moist soil and low summer temperatures. Most vigorous seedlings usually grow on exposed mineral soil, where competition of other trees and plants for available moisture may be limited. Broken soil and partial shade aids moisture retention during the critical first summer season. Perennial vegetation seems to little affect seedling growth and may, in some cases, provide moisture-conserving shade in areas of seasonal dryness.

Few coast redwood seedlings survive first year of growth. Many factors can result in seedling death, but fungi kill most on undisturbed forest floors. Lack of adequate moisture is most common in late spring and summer where seedlings have survived fungi attack. Additional causes of mortality include frost-heave on north-facing slopes and insect, bird and rodent damage. Rabbits and black-tailed deer also commonly destroy seedlings by feeding upon them.

Coast redwood seedlings are scarce in undisturbed virgin forests such as those commonly found within Redwood National Park. Such sparsity may result from lack of favorable soil conditions or from fungi which thrive in redwood forests.

Sunlight competition by mature redwoods and other forest species may contribute to seedling mortality.

Rapid growth is common in young coast redwood. Natural seedlings, however, grow slowly, often requiring three years to reach 12 inches *(30.5 cm)* in height. Vegetative sprouts, by comparison, may reach 15 inches *(38.1 cm)* or more by end of the first year. Sprouts grow more rapidly than seedlings because they draw on mature parent root systems for abundant nourishment.

Best growth of coast redwood occurs in full sunlight. Redwood may, however, endure heavy shade common to virgin stands of mature trees. Coast redwood has a remarkably efficient system for photosynthesis, conversion of light into growth nutrients. Spruce and fir species common to mature forests require nearly twice as much light as redwoods for adequate growth. Pine trees commonly require three to four times the light necessary for redwood existance.

Seedling root development is best in loose soil. In such ideal soil, young coast redwood may extend first year roots 12 inches *(30.5 cm)*. Three-inch *(7.6 cm)* deep roots are common when forest soils are compact. Most first year root development takes place during summer, when lack of moisture and warmer temperatures prompt growth.

Enemies of Coast Redwood. Mature redwood forest such as that found within Redwood National Park, is a climax, or dominant, type. When growing with other species, coast redwood is nearly always dominant. Few natural enemies affect the tall trees throughout life. The principle cause of death in redwood is fire damage. Because young seedlings and saplings do not yet have protection of the thick, fire-resistant bark common to mature trees, stands of young trees may be killed outright by ground fires. Such stands commonly retain less forest-floor moisture than mature groves, and fires are correspondingly more severe.

Old-growth stands found within Redwood National Park show evidence of three or more severe fires each century. Such fires may only serve to reduce thickness of protective, fibrous bark, and mature redwood often have thinner bark near ground than higher up their trunk. In more severe fires, injury may extend to the cambium, or growth, layer, and to the heartwood. Such fire damage may so weaken trees mechanically as to cause toppling. The damaged areas also provide entry for fungus diseases.

Two principle fungi are known by researchers to attack redwood heartwood. Such fungi commonly enter through fire scars, destroying sound heartwood and providing easily-ignited fuel for future fires. Combination of rot and fire may eventually produce large basal cavities called "goose pens." Such cavities were formerly used by early settlers of the park for poultry shelters. In extreme cases, fungal damage may cause coast redwood to fall.

Because forest fires remove less fire-resistant competition, many tree species do not occur commonly in mature forests of the park. Such alteration of plantlife succession is termed "fire-modified" or "fire-climax" forest by botanists. Researchers believe that fire prevention activities by man in preserve areas may eventually result in replacement of mature redwood stands by Douglas fir and other species.

Erosional action near park stream margins also commonly affects growth of mature trees. Such erosion serves to undermine the shallow surface roots of coast redwood and results first in leaning. Leaning redwood trees often produce vigorous growth on the affected side and form large buttress supports which serve to prop the trunk. Continued undermining by erosional waters may eventually fall such trees, however. Windstorms contribute to death of leaning trees and, in severe storms, may be primary causes of toppling. Most falling damage to mature virgin forest occurs during windstorms.

Windblown branches falling from great heights during storms pose serious hazard to park visitors. Such branches may fall at speeds over 100 miles *(161 km)* per hour and weigh many pounds. Visitors to Redwood National Park should avoid forest areas during windstorms.

Redwood enemies other than fire, wind and erosion are few in number. Coast redwood are afflicted by no tree-killing diseases, although branch canker may occasionally girdle small stems or branches. Such girdling could kill young, immature trees. Likewise, few insects commonly live upon redwoods, and none of these cause significant damage. Redwood barkbeetle may mine damaged, injured or dead trees, and larvae of twig borer occasionally burrow beneath bark in declining or dead coast redwood. Other insect pests include redwood scale, redwood mealy-bug, cypress mealy-bug, flatheaded twig borer and girdler, and Sequoia pitch moths. Of these, only Sequoia pitch moths seriously affect redwood growth. Such moths tunnel into cambium growth tissue of redwood branches and in severe infestation may cause death of young trees.

Among mammals, dusky-footed wood rats and gray squirrels may be harmful to tender sprouts and seedlings. Black bear may strip bark from trees as old as 30 years, and expose juicy sapwood which it then scrapes and chews. Such stripping may cause death of some trees, although most coast redwood damaged by bear survive injury. Small trees may also be damaged by horn polishing of blacktail deer and Roosevelt elk, common to the park. Such polishing occurs during preparation for autumn rut in these mammals, and visitors to the park may see polishing trees along hiking trails in both mixed-conifer and redwood forest.

Sapling to Maturity. Besides growing in special habitats, requiring abundant moisture and moderate temperatures, coast redwood are unique. They are long-lived, grow taller than any other known tree, and are believed exceeded in bulk only by Sierra big tree redwood of the California Sierra Nevada. In age, coast redwood mature at 400 to 500 years. Virgin redwood forests sometimes are described erroneously as "even-aged" or "over-mature." No other forest may match redwood stands for both age range and mixtures of vigorously growing and decadent trees. Park forests consist of trees ranging from less than one year to more than 1000 years in age. Visitors may see represented nearly every stage of coast redwood growth and development.

Because less than 30 per cent of redwood forest is comprised of mature, over-400 year trees, average tree size is much smaller than many first-time visitors expect. Most trees are less than 12 inches *(30.5 cm)* in diameter. Redwoods taller than 200 feet *(61 m)* are common, however. Best examples are found growing on alluvial benches located near Redwood Creek in the south and Smith River in the north. The three tallest trees of record grow in Tall Trees Grove, located about seven miles *(11.3 km)* southeast of the Orick gateway on Redwood Creek. They measure 367.8 feet *(112.1 m)*, 367.4 feet *(112.0 m)*, and 364.3 feet *(111.0 m)* respectively. Tallest is the Howard A. Libby, or Tall Tree, discovered in 1963 by Dr. Paul Zahl of the National Geographic Society. Howard Libby, for whom the tree was named, was a prominent lumberman and president of Arcata Redwood Company. Personnel of the National Park Service promote use of the name Tall Tree for popular use.

Largest diameter and height are not found in the same tree. Frank D. Stout Tree, located a short distance along Mill Creek Trail from Jedediah Smith Redwoods State Park campground, is 20 feet *(6.1 m)* diameter at chest height. It contains the largest bulk of known coast redwood found within Redwood National Park but is only 340 feet *(103.6 m)* tall.

Visitors to Redwood National Park may visit both Tall Tree Grove and Stout Tree by following route descriptions contained in the Hiking and Watercraft Trails chapter.

WILDLIFE

A wide variety of mammals, birds, reptiles and amphibians may be seen by visitors to Redwood National Park. More than 235 species of wildlife are believed living within park boundaries. Visitors may see such common and numerous animals as Roosevelt elk, raccoon, varied thrush, Oregon junco and California slender salamander. Because mature redwood forest supports few shrubs and plants and actively resists attack by insects, many species, however, are rarely seen. The best opportunities for viewing wildlife occur along streams, in meadows or in alder forest.

Wildlife Hazard. All animals within Redwood National Park are wild creatures. Visitors should exercise caution while observing or approaching such wildlife. Some larger animals may be hazardous to visitors and should be actively avoided. No serious injuries or human deaths have occurred in the park due to wildlife, but a number of household pets, especially dogs, have been killed. All dogs within the park must be supervised by a visitor and remain leashed. Pets should be kept in vehicles or tents at night and are not allowed to accompany hikers on park trails.

Rattlesnakes *(Crotalus viridus)* occur infrequently in warm inland areas of the park. Visitors who hike dry slopes and meadows within this region should carefully watch their footing.

Presence of food in campsite areas may also attract numerous pests. Park visitors should cache all food in campsite pantries, locking metal ice chests or vehicles. Raccoons are common in most areas of the park and may frequently raid food stores that are carelessly left unprotected. Raccoons can open unlocked pantries or plastic foam storage containers.

Campsite birds may also prove a nuisance to picnickers and campers. Stellar's jays *(Cyanocitta stelleri)* frequently steal food even from occupied tables. Jays are brilliant blue in color with a peaked topnotch and usually reveal their presence during early morning hours through raucous chattering.

Roosevelt Elk. Roosevelt elk *(Cervus canadensis)*, or wapiti, are large members of the deer family. Such elk are native to the park and represent a tiny fraction of once widespread herds which extended eastward to Mt. Shasta and the central California valley. Two distinct herds may be seen by visitors to Prairie Creek Redwoods State Park. One herd frequents the meadow and U.S. Highway 101 campground area, while the second lives near Gold Bluff beach. Dense coastal redwood forest separates the herds, and little mixing seems to take place.

Male elk, or bulls, develop large racks of antlers which are shed each year. Antler growth begins in spring when male elk develop tines beneath a protective covering known as velvet. Velvet provides nutrition to antlers during growth and is shed in autumn, prior to rut.

During autumn rut, Roosevelt elk band together in harem groups, dominated by a single male. Bachelor males usually remain in separate herds. Each cow bears one or two calves during late spring or early summer. Following calving, males migrate inland, leaving females and calves behind in separate herds.

Elk within Redwood National Park may sometimes appear remarkably docile or seem to ignore visitors. Despite such appearance, however, never approach closely. Bull elk during autumn are fiercely protective of cows and may charge if they feel their harem is threatened. During spring and summer, females with calves frequently become separated from their offspring while grazing. At such times, park visitors may inadvertently pass between cow and calf, provoking an attack.

Migratory patterns of park elk are the subject of studies conducted by researchers, and visitors may see animals marked with ear tags. Such studies aid biologists in determining the life history and well-being of many park animals.

Deer. Long believed by biologists a distinct species, coastal blacktail deer found within Redwood National Park have been

recently identified as a subspecies of mule deer *(Odocoileus hemionus)*. Such deer are usually smaller than mule deer found to the east, however, and may only reach maximum weights of 175 pounds *(79.4 kg)*. Like Roosevelt elk, deer rut in autumn but do not form harem groups. Usually female deer, or does, bear one or two fawns in late spring.

Deer within Redwood National Park may be seen most easily in shrub and grassland areas, or near alder forests and streams.

Best visitor observation of park deer occurs at Mill Creek campground in Del Norte Coast Redwoods State Park.

Black Bear. Black bear *(Ursus americanus)* are rarely seen by park visitors. Unlike other national parks, where high visitation and garbage have conditioned bear to associate food with man, bear within Redwood National Park are wild and usually remain hidden from sight. They have an excellent sense of smell and often detect the presence of man before being seen.

Black bear vary in color from black to cinnamon but usually have brown faces. They are normally active during nighttime hours and are omnivores, eating berries, nuts, insects, small mammals, fish and carrion. Breeding takes place during autumn, and usually two cubs are born to sows in winter dens. Rarely, as many as six may occur in a litter. Black bear cubs are blind at birth and may weigh only 12 ounces *(340 g)*. Such cubs normally remain with the sow less than one year before weaning.

WILDLIFE OF PARK FORESTS

Coast redwood forests found within Redwood National Park contain few species of wildlife. Dim light, lack of protective cover, and scarcity of abundant food makes such forest unattractive to most animals. Only when meadows create openings, where redwood yields to Sitka spruce and Douglas fir, or where border areas permit vegetative growth, are many species of animals common.

Most easily seen mammals living within coastal forests of the park are squirrels. Douglas squirrels, or chickaree *(Tamiasciurus douglasi)*, are small in size with a dark brown back and have small tails with no white hair. Chickaree feed on seeds and cones of Douglas fir. Western gray squirrels *(Sciurus griseus)*, may be found in park tanoak forests where they feed on acorns and fungi. They are much larger than chickaree, have totally gray bodies and full, bushy tails. Northern flying squirrels *(Glaucomys sabrinus)* may also live within Redwood National Park, but no sure identifications have been made. All three squirrels build tree-trunk nests in enlarged woodpecker holes. Large nests of coarse sticks seen atop some park trees mark the homes of dusky-footed wood rat *(Neotoma fuscipes)*, an herbivore which feeds on seeds, nuts, acorns, green vegetation and fungi. Such animals may be quite large, occasionally weighing .5 pound *(227 g)* or more. Often seen nearby in trees of Douglas fir are the smaller nests of red tree mice *(Arborimus longicaudus)*. Such mice eat young foliage and build their nests of needles around a core of aromatic resin. Dwellings of red tree mice may pleasantly scent the forest air on warm sunny days.

Because birds are not plentiful in coast redwood forests, or may live high in crowns of mature coast redwood, they are often difficult to observe. Two species, however, are common. Varied thrush *(Ixoreus naevius)* are robin-sized birds that are attractively marked with orange, black and brown. Winter wrens *(Troglodytes troglodytes)* are small, brown birds which prefer dark, damp forest habitats. Such wrens eat insects and spiders. Other species of birdlife occasionally seen in coast redwood forest include warblers, owls, juncos, sparrows and woodpeckers.

Amphibians are most widespread among the wildlife creatures found in mature park forests. Amphibians require water for breeding in springtime, but may migrate widely throughout the park during other seasons. Such animals usually live in moist habitats that include rotting logs and bark, or beneath leaves and litter of the forest floor.

Salamanders and newts are the most numerous amphibians found within Redwood National Park. Among moist or rotten wood on the forest floor, visitors may see California slender salamander *(Batrachoceps attenuatus)*, with narrow bodies and tiny, short legs. Slender salamander are usually less than three inches *(7.6 cm)* long, and are colored with a broad, tan marking extending from head to tail.

Rough-skinned newts *(Taricha granulosa)* may occasionally be observed crawling on moist earth beneath forest vegetation. More commonly, visitors may view such amphibians under water of slow-moving streams, ponds and puddles. Rough-skinned newts are usually brown with a yellow to red underside.

WILDLIFE OF PARK STREAMS

Large streams and rivers found within Redwood National Park provide homes for many species of wildlife not common elsewhere in the park. Major waterways, such as Klamath and Smith rivers and Redwood and Mill creeks, provide best opportunity for viewing mammals, birds, amphibians, and reptiles of park streams. Visitors may best view such animals at Prairie Creek Redwoods State Park and Del Norte Coast Redwoods State Park.

Birds. Among birds, water ouzel *(Cinclus mexicanus)*, or dippers, spend most of their life near torrents of rushing water. Such birds may be easily identified by their characteristic bobbing motion and gray foliage. Ouzels frequently dive, swim underwater, and walk on the bottom of streams while feeding on aquatic insects. At such times, they swim with graceful, yet powerful sweeps of their wings and guide their motion with strong, water-repellent tail feathers. Ouzels nest on streamside rock walls, often within a few feet of water.

Also common near park streams are spotted sandpipers *(Actitus macularia).* Sandpipers are olive-brown above and white or cream below. In summer, such birds have rounded, black spots on their breast. Sandpipers construct shallow, grass-lined nests near river shores and walk with a characteristic teetering motion.

Visitors to the park may occasionally see flocks of great blue heron *(Ardea herodias)* with large broad wings, crook-shaped necks and long, trailing legs. Heron are slate gray to dull blue and may reach lengths of four feet *(1.2 m)* or more. They have sharp, dagger-like bills used for catching small fish, frogs and salamanders, and occasionally fly great distances inland.

Wood ducks *(Aix sponsa)* are rarely seen by park visitors. Wood ducks build their nests in trees and atop rocky platforms near park streams and are usually seen flying in groups along river courses. They are magnificently colored with feathers ranging from brilliant red to vibrant blue.

Roosting atop branches which overhang park rivers and streams, visitors may occasionally see belted kingfisher *(Megaceryle alcyon).* Such birds are quite small, are blue, and have sharp, short bills used for catching fish. They frequently dive from their perch into the water with remarkable speed, often emerging with fish or aquatic amphibians larger than themselves.

Mammals. Park streams and rivers also provide homes to a variety of mammals, including river otter, beaver and mountain beaver.

Beaver *(Castor canadensis)* may be found throughout the water system of Redwood National Park. Beaver found within Redwood National Park are not native to the area but were introduced during transplanting operations conducted by the California State Department of Fish and Game during World War II.

Best opportunities for viewing these shy rodents occur along Klamath and Smith rivers and near Redwood and Mill creeks. Hikers of Mill Creek Trail may see felled alder and willow used by beaver for food. Beavers found within the park do not build stick houses common to beaver of other areas. Instead, they tunnel into cut banks of streams, building dwellings which may withstand winter periods of high water. Beaver dams are rarely seen.

River otter *(Lutra canadensis)* may reach lengths of three feet *(.9 m)*, are dark brown in color and have thick, tapering tails used while swimming. Otter are close relatives of weasel and primarily feed on fish. Salmon-rearing ponds of Prairie Creek Fish Hatchery, located on U.S. Highway 101, 2.5 miles *(4 km)* south of Prairie Creek Redwoods State Park campground, have been invaded by river otters several times.

River otter of Redwood National Park may be observed occasionally in ocean mouths of rivers and streams or even some distance to sea. At such times they are frequently mistaken for sea otter, a different species.

Mountain beaver *(Aplodontia rufa)*, or boomers, are distant relatives of true beaver. Most biologists believe they are the most primitive living rodent. Mountain beaver resemble tailless muskrats and frequently dig burrows beneath tangles of low brush or vines near streams. Such burrows may be six inches *(15 cm)* or more in diameter and resemble dwellings of gophers. Mountain beaver occur naturally in Northern California and may range as far northward as British Columbia.

Amphibians. Several species of frogs and salamanders are common to park streams, ponds and rivers. Yellow-legged frogs *(Rana boylei)* are most common near small ponds of quiet water. Red-legged frogs *(Rana aurora)* usually prefer briskly moving streams. Pacific tree frogs *(Hyla regilla)*, by comparison, may be found throughout the park. They are common in meadows, forests, streamsides and even grasses and shrubs near park beaches. Adult tree frogs are usually green but may also be brown or spotted. Small, adhesive discs on their toes allow them to climb when necessary.

Fishermen may occasionally catch larvae of Pacific giant salamander *(Dicamptodon ensatus)* while angling in small streams for trout or salmon. Such larvae often reach lengths of 12 inches *(30.5 cm)*. Adult Pacific giant salamanders are smaller, usually less than six inches *(15.2 cm)*. Such adults appear marbled and are one of the few salamanders known to emit sounds. When molested, they produce a low-pitched grunt of displeasure.

WILDLIFE OF PARK MEADOWS AND SHRUBLANDS

Meadows and shrublands of Redwood National Park are frequently small areas within coast redwood forests or near the sea. Visitors to the park may most easily view wildlife of meadow and shrublands near Gold Bluff beach campground in Prairie Creek Redwoods State Park. Many species of birds and mammals are common in these areas.

Birds. Among birds, the most common inhabitants of park meadows are swallows. Barn swallows *(Hirundo rustica)* and violet-green swallows *(Tachycinetta thalassima)* visit the park by summer, then migrate southward in winter. Both may be seen flying low over grasslands in search of insects. Barn swallows may be identified by their orange chest and forked tail, while violet-green swallows have a white chest and square tail.

Nearby, Oregon juncos *(Junco oreganus)* may be identified by their distinctive dark gray to black head, gray back and white underside. They frequently feed with song sparrows *(Melospiza melodia)*, rufous-sided towhees *(Pipilo erythroph-*

thalmus) and slate-colored juncos *(Junco hyemalis)*. Unlike sparrows, however, juncos feed primarily on seeds of perennial grasses.

Small plump bodies and distinctive markings help identify chestnut-backed chickadees *(Parus rufescens)*. Chickadees are brown, have black heads and white cheeks, and may suspend themselves from branches and twigs at all angles while searching for berries and seeds.

Two hummingbird species frequent Redwood National Park during spring and summer. Allen's hummingbird *(Selasphorus sasin)* migrates to the park during February and March and may be identified by its iridescent green back and bright orange-red throat. Seen more rarely within the park are rufous humming-birds *(Selasphorus rufus)*. Male rufous hummingbirds are rust-colored, but females resemble those of Allen's humming-bird. Hummingbirds are acrobatic fliers and position themselves by adjustment of wing and tail feathers. They may hover, dart, swoop and even fly backwards. In spring, Allen's hummingbirds mate, and visitors may see male birds fly in great U-shaped arcs while feathers of their tail emit shrill buzzing sounds. Such displays often attract female birds.

Mammals. Mammals common to park meadows and shrublands include deer, bear, raccoon, spotted skunk, porcupine and numerous rodents. Deer are close relatives of elk but do not form harem groups during rut. They also lack the long throat manes common to elk, and form antlers with forked tines. Deer may be seen most easily during early morning and evening hours.

Raccoons *(Procyon lotor)* are most active at night when they may be seen by campers in Prairie Creek Redwoods and Del Norte Coast Redwoods state parks. Raccoons are large animals with dark markings ringing their tails and marking their faces. They are omnivores and eat a wide variety of meat, fish and plantlife.

Two species of skunk are common within Redwood National Park. Most frequently seen by visitors are spotted skunks *(Spilogale putorius)*, distinguished by their black body and four, broken white stripes. Spotted skunks may stand on their front feet when cornered and extend their hind legs and tail in warn-

ing. At such times, white hairs of the tail are spread and appear as a white rosette. Few park visitors will twice ignore the warning signal of spotted skunks. When provoked further, skunks exude a powerful scent from glands located near the base of their tail.

Also common within the park are striped skunks *(Mephitis mephitis)*. Similar in size and appearance to house cats, striped skunks have a brilliant white blaze on their face which divides into two parallel stripes on the back and tail. Visitors most frequently detect the presence of both varieties of skunks by their distinctive odor.

Porcupine *(Erethizon dorsatum)* are recent additions to Redwood National Park. Continuous growth of young trees following logging in recently forested areas first attracted such animals to the park. Porcupine are large and clumsy, and are covered by long, barbed spines, or quills. Such quills are not thrown as is popularly believed, but are loosely attached. Only accidental brushing of a porcupine may result in penetration of skin. Visitors should take care to avoid such encounters.

Most common among park meadow and shrubland residents are Townsend's chipmunk *(Eutamias townsendi)*. Visitors may identify this small rodent by alternately dark and light side stripes. Townsend's chipmunk are active during daylight hours when they feed on, and store, seeds. Cheek pouches of chipmunks are often distended with food.

WILDLIFE OF OCEAN AND SHORELINE

Near shorelines of Redwood National Park, visitors may see wildlife not visible elsewhere, including whales, sea lions, seals, sea otter and numerous birds. Best locations for viewing such animals occur at Nickel Creek campground, south of the Crescent City gateway, and Gold Bluff beach in Prairie Creek Redwoods State Park.

Sea lions are common mammals on rocky park shorelines. They are carnivores and feed on a variety of fish and crustacean life, and may be identified by their great size and dark brown to black color. Two species are common within the park. Steller, or northern, sea lions *(Eumetopias jubata)* are very large, and males often reach weights of 2000 pounds *(908 kg)* or more. Such sea lions may be identified by their low forehead and loud, barking call when disturbed or mating. Steller sea lions form herds when mating. They may dive to great depths when feeding, sometimes more than 80 fathoms *(146 m)*. California sea lions *(Zalophus californianus)* are much smaller, seldom weighing more than 600 pounds *(272 kg)*. They have a high forehead and emit a continual honking bark. Visitors to the park may have seen such sea lions as performing "seals." Both species may fish in large rivers and lagoons of the park during autumn runs of salmon.

Harbor seals *(Phoca vitulina)* may frequently be seen by park visitors. Unlike sea lions, seals may vary from black to light gray and are very curious. Seals often approach humans in boats and on shore within 100 feet *(30.5 m)*. Their legs have adapted to life within the sea and form fluke-like tails. Seals are clumsy on land, where they must drag their flippers behind them. Harbor seals may invade rivers for many miles while feeding on salmon, steelhead and trout.

During spring and fall migrations, thousands of gray whales *(Eschrichtius glaucus)* pass nearby Redwood National Park, enroute to Baja California or north to the Arctic. Atop high bluffs such as Crescent Bay Overlook, 2.7 miles *(4.3 km)* south of Crescent City, visitors may see spouts of gray whales. In shallow water, they are blotchy gray in appearance and may reach lengths of 50 feet *(15.2 m)*. Their coloration results from barnacle scars dotting their thick skin.

While breathing, gray whales spout streams of water and moist air 20 feet *(6.1 m)* or more into the air. Such spouts often occur in groups of three or more, then cease for long periods as the whale dives, or sounds, to great depths. Gray whales lack true teeth and feed, instead, on microscopic plankton and plants found in sea water. Filtering great quantities of water through baleen plates hanging vertically from the roof of the mouth, such whales collect more than two tons *(1814 kg)* of food daily.

Many smaller dolphins, porpoises and killer whales may be seen by park seashore visitors. Pacific white-sided dolphin, Dall and harbor porpoise and killer whales feed in shallow waters near the coast.

Most conspicuous among seabirds found within Redwood National Park are sea gulls. Several species, including western, Heermann's, California, and glaucous-winged gulls *(Larus spp.)*, frequent park shores and rivers. Gulls are omnivores and feed on carrion, mollusks, fish and marine plants. Such birds exhibit effortless, soaring flight.

Other marine birds include cormorants, pelicans and numerous species of duck. Cormorants *(Phalacrocorax spp.)* are large, black birds usually seen resting in lagoon, shore and river waters. Its bill is long, with a pronounced hook. Cormorants frequently fly awkwardly, holding their heads far ahead of the body and flapping without pause. Pelicans *(Pelecanus occidentalis)* are best seen near Freshwater Lagoon, 2.5 miles *(4 km)* west of the Orick gateway. Such birds frequently fly in V-shaped lines for great distances. When feeding, they climb to great heights, fold their wings and dive beneath water. Throughout autumn and winter, ducks enroute south may be seen in nearby marshes and ponds.

Included among shorebirds are black oyster catcher, willet, black turnstone and sanderling. Black oyster catchers *(Haemotopus bachmani)* may be identified by their pale legs and long, reddish bill. Oyster catchers feed on crabs, clams and other marine animals. Turnstones *(Arenaria melanocephala)* are common along the water edge, where they bob for sand fleas and tiny animals.

Visitors wishing to closely view marine birdlife should carry binoculars, as close approach on foot is frequently made impossible by rugged terrain.

Within the boundaries of Redwood National Park, visitors may see a wide panorama of plant communities, ranging from cathedral stands of redwood on river flats to ground-hugging plants scattered among driftwood logs of coastal beaches. Mixed-conifer forests clothe slopes and ridges while evergreen and broad-leaved trees grow abundantly in recently-forested areas. Visitors to seaward hillsides and bluffs may find weedy invaders from Europe and South America, mixed with native plants used for food by early settlers.

Plantlife of Redwood National Park includes many species. For convenience of visitors, this guidebook classifies such plants in six easily-seen categories. Within these groups one may easily explore the flora of the park.

PLANTS OF COAST REDWOOD FORESTS

Trees and Shrubs. The best examples of mature redwood forest in Redwood National Park may be seen by visitors to Tall Tree Grove, seven miles *(11.3 km)* southeast of the Orick gateway; John Irvine-Miners Ridge Loop in Prairie Creek Redwoods State Park; and Frank D. Stout Grove within Jedediah Smith Redwoods State Park. Other evergreen cone-bearing trees occur occasionally within such groves, but coast redwood *(Sequoia sempervirens)* typically dominates park forests. Visitors may distinguish coast redwood from other conifers of the park by its thick, reddish-brown bark which is fibrous and deeply furrowed. Both redwood bark and wood are extremely fire resistant until cut and seasoned, and fallen trees may lie for centuries on forest floors before being destroyed by rot.

Leaves of coast redwood are about one inch *(2.5 cm)* long, broad, flat and pointed. Such leaves are arranged in sprays with distinct upper and lower orientation. Leaves from atop coast redwood trees, however, are often quite different in appearance. Such leaves react to abundant sunlight and are awl-shaped. They may remind visitors of leaves found on Sierra big tree redwood *(Sequoiadendron giganteum)*.

Redwood cones are oblong in shape and about one inch *(2.5 cm)* in diameter. Scales of such cones do not overlap as familiar in pine trees. Instead, each scale is fastened in a circular band to the central stalk, much like tiny umbrellas. The scales open during the winter months and shower the forest floor with tiny, winged seeds. The cones are attached to a short stalk and later fall to the ground. In addition to seed, redwoods may reproduce by sprouts, which develop when damaged by fire, flooding, or other disaster occurs. Many examples exist of sprouts forming rings around parent trees. Such rings eventually grow circular groves of trees found commonly within the park.

Visitors seeking additional information on growth and development of coast redwood should refer to the Coast Redwoods chapter.

Streamside coast redwood forest near the Pacific Ocean often includes Sitka spruce *(Picea sitchensis)*. Spruce may be distinguished from other park trees by their characteristic corn-flake patterned bark, sharp, short needles and two-inch *(5 cm)* cones comprised of papery, overlapping scales. Sitka spruce is common in rain forests of Olympic National Park, located to the north in the State of Washington.

Beneath tall conifers, a poorly-developed layer of shrubs may by seen by park visitors. Due to lack of adequate light, plants of this layer seldom grow to large size. Western azalea *(Rhododendron occidentale)* is the most attractive and common such shrub. Azalea grow in moist spots within redwood forest and flower in spring. The large, attractive flowers of azalea are creamy-yellow to pale pink, depending both on particular plant and light conditions. Two species of azalea are native within California.

Another shrub common to redwood forests is California laurel *(Umbellularia californica)*, also known as bay or pepperwood. When light conditions are sufficiently strong laurel sometimes may grow as medium-sized trees. The strongly aromatic leaves of California laurel are widely used as a seasoning and are sold commercially as bay leaves.

Herbs and Ferns. Herbs and ferns are common associates of shrubs on redwood forest floors. Most such herbs are perennial, spring blooming and white-flowered. They are abundant within the park and often begin flowering during the rainy mid-winter period. Long before arrival of most visitors, the unusual brown flowers of slink pod *(Scoliopus bigelovii)*, a relative of lily, have bloomed and died. Fruit of slink pod form on stems which elongate and push their seeds beneath ground. Another early park wildflower is cross-shaped showy toothwart *(Dentaria californica)*. Toothworts are related to garden mustards and have margins with coarse teeth.

As spring progresses, redwood violet *(Viola sempervirens)* become prominent with fragrant yellow flowers and evergreen, heart-shaped leaves. Because the leaves of wild ginger *(Asarum caudatum)* are also heart-shaped, visitors may occasionally confuse it with redwood violet. The fragrant, velvety leaves and brownish, tailed flowers hidden below the leaves of ginger, however, quickly distinguish the two. While wild ginger is not the same as that purchased commercially, it has always been popular among edible wild plant enthusiasts.

Still later in spring, displays of multi-colored wildflowers burst from stems and bulbs hidden below ground. Showiest of redwood forest bulbed plants is wake robin *(Trillium ovatum)*. Its conspicuous, white, three-parted flowers rise above three leaves on their common stalk. Flowers of wake robin fade to veined purple with age.

Flowers of the lily family are well represented in park forests. False lily of the valley *(Maianthemum dilatatum)* is an unusual example with four-parted flowers. Broad leaves, which include curved veins, serve to distinguish these plants. The white flowers of false lily of the valley yield small red berries in summer. Another member of the lily family is false Solomon's seal *(Smilacina amplexicaule)*, which grows a single, arching stem scattered with leaves along its length. Flowers of false Solomon's seal are small and numerous and later produce berries. Such flowers are similar to neighboring fairy bells *(Disporum hookeri and Disporum smithii).* Fairy bells display a few cream-colored flowers that hang on forked stems beneath the plant. Visitors may distinguish the two fairy bell species common to Redwood National Park by examining their leaves. One fairy bell has smooth leaves; the other is covered with fine hairs.

Most plentiful plant of Redwood National Park forests is redwood sorrel *(Oxalis oregona).* It covers the ground in extensive mats with three-parted clover-like leaves which are green above and red beneath. Leaves of redwood sorrel contain slight amounts of oxalic acid, which impart to it a tart flavor. The recent popularity of edible wild foods has made sorrel a common ingredient in several delightful recipes. In spring its plants bear white to light pink flowers.

Bleeding heart *(Dicentra formosa)* is a common herb which grows among ferns on moist stream banks. Its leaves are somewhat fleshy and much divided. Pink heart-shaped flowers hang in clusters from arching stems above the leaves. In other parts of the United States similar species are referred to as Dutchman's breeches, a fanciful reference to the shape of its flowers.

Commonly associated with bleeding heart is fringe cup *(Tolmeia grandiflora).* Visitors should observe flowers of fringe cup closely to appreciate their delicate growth of feathery pink petals which emerge from tiny green cups. Later, fruits split open to reveal shiny black seeds. Nearby, small herbs grow with strap-shaped, fleshy leaves and pink, five-petalled flowers. Such herbs are close relatives of spring beauty *(Claytonia virginica),* common to the eastern United States.

In late spring and early summer, bright wildflower colors fade and the redwood forest becomes muted with shades of green. Visitors to the park at this time may easily view trail plant *(Adenocaulon bicolor).* When disturbed, such plants commonly expose silvery leaf undersides. Visitors may also search for a minute member of the orchid family, disguised both by its size and color. Rattlesnake plantain *(Goodyera oblongifolia)* may be recognized by its minute, green flowers and darker, silver-striped leaves. Such leaves may be more easily seen before the rattlesnake plantain flowers bloom. In autumn, seed pods of plantain dry and rattle in forest wind,

prompting its common name.

Several species of fern grace terraces and moist banks of mature redwood forest. Perhaps most distinctive is maidenhair fern *(Adiantum pedatum)*. Leaflets of maidenhair fern are fan-shaped, with folded margins, while its stems are forked and shiny black. Most other common park ferns have regular leaf-lets lining their unbranched stems. The abundant sword fern *(Polystichum munitum)* may be easily distinguished by tiny ears found at the base of each leaflet. Smaller deer fern *(Blechnum spicant)* fronds lack separate leaflets and ears.

Two other ferns are common to the park but not easily rec-ognized by visitors. Both have triangular, many-lobed fronds. They are shield *(Dryopteris dilatata)* and lady fern *(Athyrium filix-femina)*.

PLANTS OF SLOPE FORESTS

On slopes and ridges of Redwood National Park, the forest changes both in composition and character. On such sites, coast redwood mix growth with several other trees including Douglas fir, western hemlock, tanoak and madrone. Bald Hills road forest, including trees of Lady Bird Johnson Grove, and roadside forest seen near U.S. Highway 101 in Del Norte Coast Redwoods State Park are best park examples of slope redwood forests.

Mature Douglas fir *(Pseudotsuga menziesii)* growing within the park rival slope coast redwood both in size and age. Visitors may recognize Douglas fir by their light brown, deeply fur-rowed bark. Needles of fir are usually soft, blunt, and make fine, aromatic herbal tea. Fir buds are large and pointed, and visitors may distinguish cones by their three-pointed, papery bracts, or modified leaves, which emerge from between scales. Like coast redwood, Douglas fir is commonly harvested com-mercially.

Western hemlock *(Tsuga heterophylla)* may be identified at some distance by their characteristic drooping tops, especially when young. Foliage of hemlock include flat sprays of needles comprised of individual leaves of different lengths. Cones are small and somewhat resemble Douglas fir and Sitka spruce.

Although commonly seen along roads and trails in many areas of the park, western hemlock is not as abundant in slope forests as Douglas fir or redwood. It most often occurs as growth atop fallen redwood logs, and visitors may notice its straddling, octopus-like roots. Beneath the canopy of slope evergreen conifers, broad-leaved tanoak and madrone may be seen. Tanoak *(Lithocarpus densiflora)* is a relative of the true oaks and produces, like them, acorn fruit. As its common name suggests, these trees provide a source for leather tanning agents, and its bark is collected commercially.

Visitors may distinguish madrone *(Arbutus menziesii)* by its distinctive bright red bark. During summer months, large patches of such bark may peel away from new growth, exposing lighter wood. Madrone wood is hard and durable but is difficult to work because of warping. Leathery, evergreen leaves and displays of white, urn-shaped flowers suggest its relationship to manzanitas of California chaparral. In late fall madrone produces vast quantities of edible, though warty, red berries.

Shrubs. Shrub growth in slope forests of the park is more widely populated than that of mature redwood stands common near creeks and rivers. Several shrubs found growing in slope forests are related to madrone. California rose-bay *(Rhododendron macrophyllum)* has large leathery leaves and beautiful clusters of showy violet to pink flowers which form to highlight the late spring blooming period. Rose-bay is related to western azalea and is locally termed rhododendron. Salal *(Gaultheria shallon)* is a smaller park shrub with zig-zag stems and leathery leaves. Salal is commonly harvested with sword ferns for use in floral arrangements. The shrub bears small pink blossoms similar to flowers of madrone and huckleberry. The fleshy, purple fruits are edible but nearly tasteless.

California huckleberry *(Vaccinium ovatum)* is an unusual evergreen shrub with shiny leaves. It may produce its pink, urn-shaped flowers as early as mid-winter. Visitors will find the small black fruit of huckleberry, which matures in late summer and fall, delicious eating. Red huckleberry *(Vaccinium parvifolium)* is a close relative with small, deciduous leaves that are translucent. Such leaves grow on sharply-angled stems and, in fall, red huckleberry produces a tasty red fruit. Oregon grape *(Berberis nervosa)* is the only common shrub of the park with large spiny leaflets. Although sometimes spindley in appearance, plants found in the park are usually low-growing and well-formed. The small, yellow flowers of Oregon grape grow from stalks near centers of the leaves. Its blue, seedy berries make excellent jelly.

Leaves of hazelnut, or filbert *(Corylus cornuta)* are fuzzy, coarsely toothed, and asymmetrical. Their fruit is an edible nut, surrounded by cup-shaped, papery envelopes. Hazelnut tends to blend with other shrubs during summer months but is easily distinguished by drooping cylindrical flower clusters when winter approaches. Such flowers bloom in vivid contrast to stark, barren limbs. Local Native Americans have used the young and flexible twigs of hazelnut in basketry.

Wild honeysuckle *(Lonicera hispidula)*, a relative of cultivated garden ornamentals, occurs within Redwood National Park as a vine with small opposite leaves, scrambling over other plants. It commonly yields fragrant clusters of flowers during early spring.

Herbs. Herbs of slope forests are not as abundant, nor as common as in redwood forests of alluvial river plains. Possibly most visible to visitors during May and June is leopard lily *(Lilium pardalinum)*. Large, orange, spotted flowers of leopard lily are unmistakable components of slope forest floors. It is most common along U.S. 101 in Del Norte Coast Redwoods State Park. Native iris *(Iris douglasiana)* bloom most commonly in April and May. Iris plants form large clumps with many blue, small to medium-sized flowers. They most commonly occur in meadow openings and pastures.

Hedge nettle *(Stachys emersonii)* commonly grows pairs of opposite leaves on its square stem. The red flowers of hedge nettles may remind visitors of garden mint, a relation. While many members of the mint family have a pleasing odor, the aroma of hedge nettle may be faintly unpleasant. Such nettle does not carry, however, the unpleasant stings of common stinging nettle.

Two species of inside-out flower exist in the park; one with deciduous leaves *(Vancouveria hexandra)*, the other *(Vancou-*

veria planipetala), an evergreen. Both plants are aptly named for the white petals of their blossoms which turn backwards strongly. The generic scientific name commemorates George Vancouver, an early British explorer who sailed the Pacific northwest. Sweet Cicely *(Osmorhiza purpurea),* a relative of carrot, often remains unnoticed in park forests. Its curved, seed-like fruits, however, often stick to socks and pantlegs. Cicely yields a licorice odor when crushed due to anise contained within its leaves.

PLANTS OF THE ALDER FORESTS

Some forest regions within Redwood National Park contain few redwood trees and are clothed instead with alder, cottonwood and willows. Red alder *(Alnus oregana)* is a medium-sized tree with gray-white bark. Its flowers are small and very specialized. Such flowers cluster and resemble small, brown, woody cones less than one inch *(2.5 cm)* long. These cones remain on alder long after release of their seed.

Visitors to the park may recognize black cottonwood *(Populus trichocarpa)* by its triangular leaves. Cottonwood flowers usually bloom during winter and later produce clustered fruits filled with cottony seeds. Such seeds blow in great profusion through many areas of the park. A close relative of cottonwood is willow *(Salix spp.).* Many species of willow occur in Redwood National Park. Such trees may be recognized by numerous buds covered by single bud scales. Visitors who wish to distinguish the varied species of willow occurring in the park will require a proper field guide. Two such botanical guides to park trees are:

A California Flora, *by P. A. Munz in collaboration with D. Keck. (University of California, Berkeley: 1959).*

A Field Guide To Trees and Shrubs, *by G. A. Petrides. (Houghton & Mifflin Company, Boston, Massachusetts: 1958).*

Associated with alder, cottonwood and willow are trees of bigleaf maple *(Acer macrophyllum)*. Bigleaf maple has opposite leaves with five to seven pointed lobes and is used by Canada as a national symbol. Its fruit resembles small propellor blades. Maple of Redwood National Park may be tapped for sugar during spring, but sap flow in milder climate areas is commonly weak.

Branches of bigleaf maple are often draped with mosses and lichens and provide ideal habitats for growth of leather *(Polypodium scouleri)* and licorice ferns *(Polypodium glycyrrhiza)*. These fern species may be distinguished from each other by leatheriness of fronds; licorice fern has a filmy, translucent leaf blade. Beneath park maples, visitors may occasionally view large chain fern *(Woodwardia fimbriata)*, whose light green fronds may reach lengths exceeding six feet *(1.8 m)*. The common name for chain fern originates in repeating patterns of brown spots on its leaves, formed by clusters of spore cases.

Wetter sites also provide ideal habitats for giant horsetail *(Equisetum telmateia)*. In early spring, horsetail produce simple, cone-bearing stems. Later in the season, however, second stems emerge with whorls of green, leaf-like branches. Such second stems contain silica within their tissue, and early settlers used them for scouring soiled cooking utensils.

Western skunk cabbage *(Lysichiton americanum)* also may be found in areas of standing water. Leaves of this plant are yellow-green and leathery. Skunk cabbage is a close relative of philodendron and cala-lily and has winter blooming flowers. Such flowers cluster on a thick, club-shaped stalk and are partially surrounded by an enveloping yellow leaf. The foul, penetrating odor of skunk cabbage allows little doubt as to source of its common name. Like most members of its family, skunk cabbage is toxic due to crystals of calcium oxalate imbedded within its tissues.

PLANTS OF FORESTED HILLS AND ROADSIDES

Many areas within Redwood National Park were forested by timber firms before establishment of the preserve. Such regions are now covered by young forests of alder, Douglas fir, coast redwood, and many shrubs and weedy herbs. One of the most common spring-blooming shrubs is red-flowering currant (*Ribes sanguineum*). Currant flowers before its small leaves have completely opened. Less easily seen by visitors is gooseberry (*Ribes roezlii*), with red spiny fruits in summer months.

Thimbleberry, salmonberry, Himalaya berry and California blackberry are very common shrubs of forested hillsides and may be seen by visitors throughout much of the park. Most distinctive is salmonberry (*Rubus spectabilis*), a thorny-stemmed shrub with red-petalled flowers and salmon-colored fruit. Leaves of salmonberry are three-parted and typical of this group of woody plants. The mild flavor of salmonberry fruit, however, may be disappointing to many visitors.

Thimbleberry (*Rubus parviflorus*) has a simple, maple-like leaf. Its fruit is a raspberry and separates easily from the stem. California blackberry (*Rubus vitifolius*) grows on a thorny vine. Unlike thimbleberry, its fruit does not separate easily from its stalk.

Five-parted leaves distinguish Himalaya berry (*Rubus procerus*) from native blackberry. The fruit of Himalaya berry is large and tasty, though juicy. Vines of both black and Himalaya berry form huge briar patches which may prove impenetrable to hikers.

Unrelated to other park berries is elderberry (*Sambucus callicarpa*), a relative of honeysuckle. Elderberry leaves are divided into several leaflets and grow in pairs, opposite the stem. Its white-creamy flowers are small but cluster into easily-visible, dense masses. Elderberry form red, clustered fruit in summer and are suitable for making of wine. Plants are occasionally toxic, but poisoning in humans and cattle is rare.

Blue blossom (*Ceanothus thrysiflorus*) grow in large bushes with green stems and small leaves. In spring, blue blossom is easily visible because of its masses of sky blue flowers. It often colonizes bare areas and provides soil with nitrogen for future forest development.

Ocean spray (*Holodiscus discolor*) is aptly named, but not restricted in growth to seaside habitats. Visitors to the park may often find its clusters of tiny, cream-white flowers that resemble froth on ocean waves. Ocean spray is particularly common along U.S. Highway 101 in Del Norte County, south of the

Crescent City gateway.

Two shrubs provide brilliant red color to late park summer and fall days. Vine maple *(Acer circinatum)* is a close relative of bigleaf maple and is common along the roadside of U.S. Highway 101, north of Orick. Visitors may touch vine maple without fear but should take special care to avoid nearby poison oak *(Toxicodendron diversilobum)*. Like eastern poison ivy and sumac relatives, poison oak may cause severe inflammation and itching discomfort in sensitive individuals. Visitors may quickly recognize this colorful, if potentially hazardous, fall plant by its three-parted variable leaflets. In spring and early summer, poison oak is rich green in color. All parts of the plant, with possible exception of pollen grains, are toxic and should be avoided.

On warmer days during summer, the air of park meadows is often filled with the distinctive odor of coyote bush *(Baccharis pilularis)*. This rounded shrub is a member of the sunflower family. Its inconspicuous flowers are tiny by contrast to sunflowers, however, and may be overlooked even when in full bloom. In late fall and winter coyote bush develops white-plummed fruits.

Regions of the park which have been forested contain several characteristic herbs. First to appear in spring is coltsfoot *(Petasites palmatum)*. The pink to white flower clusters common of coltsfoot usually appear before first leaves. Such leaf blades are attached at their middle to the leaf stalk. Coltsfoot is followed closely by the yellow, waxy flowers of buttercup *(Ranunculus spp.)*. Most common to park visitors is an introduced species *(Ranunculus repens)*. Buttercups commonly grow in wet sites. Leaves of buttercup are acrid, and if eaten in quantity, may produce discomfort.

During summer, ox-eye daisy *(Chrysanthemum leucanthemum)* grow abundantly along park roadsides. Flowers of ox-eye daisy are nearly 1.5 inches *(3.8 cm)* in diameter and have bright yellow centers with white, radiating straps. Such flowers were first introduced from Europe but are found today in many areas of northern California. Ox-eye daisy sometimes occurs with its relation, yarrow *(Achillea millefolium)*. Visitors may easily distinguish yarrow by its feathery, fern-like foliage and flat-topped, white flower clusters. Yarrow yields a distinctive odor similar to sage when crushed. The scientific name for yarrow is believed based on mythical use of this healing herb by Achilles.

Also found along park roadsides are four-parted, red-pink flowers of fireweed *(Epilobium angustifolium)*. Fireweed grows widely throughout the world, and visitors may find plants as distant as the Rockies, Alaska or even Europe and Asia. Growing even more widespread is bracken fern *(Pteridium aquilinum)*. It typically has large triangular, somewhat brittle fronds, or leaves. Young, rolled-up leaves of bracken fern, or fiddleheads, have long been popular edible wild plants. Bracken fern is also quite toxic and may cause death in horses and cattle. The toxic agent is weak, however, and humans seldom eat sufficient quantities for concern.

Very large, plummed pampas grass *(Cortaderia atacamensis)*, introduced from South America, has invaded many roadsides and forested redwood hillsides. Such grass is unusual, for single plants may produce either seed or pollen, but not both. Plants found in Redwood National Park thus may be all female and able to seed without benefit of male plants.

PLANTS OF NORTHCOAST SHRUBLANDS AND BEACHES

Plantlife of the northcoast shrub community includes many species found elsewhere in Redwood National Park. Visitors may explore such shrublands where forest and tree communities yield to low plants and grass on near-coastal bluffs and seaside slopes of the park. Alder and Sitka spruce near the sea are often shaped and pruned by salt spray and wind into picturesque sculptures popular with photographers. Salt and wind effects may also create dense thickets impassible to even most determined hikers.

Very early among shrubland blooming plants is silk tassel *(Garrya elliptica)*. Silk tassel has leathery, opposite leaves and long, greenish flowers which later bear pendant clusters of black berries. Both flowers and berries are covered with silky hairs.

Shrubland California wax myrtle *(Myrica californica)* has fragrant gray-green, oblong leaves and clusters of small, purple fruits, covered by dull wax. Wax myrtle is frequently used as a fragrance source for Christmas bay candles.

Also common to shrubland areas of the park are artemisia and wild cucumber. A relative of desert sagebrush, artemisia *(Artemisia suksdorfii)* usually grows with coarsely-toothed leaves colored green above and silver below. Artemisia is more commonly seen by visitors in summer and fall than during other seasons. Wild cucumber, or man root *(Marah oreganus)*, grows with trailing vines and lobed, shiny leaves. Root of wild cucumber may grow to massive size, and occasionally plants reach 150 pounds *(68 kg)*. During autumn, small white flowers of such cucumbers develop prickly green fruit with large seeds.

Beaches. Beaches of Redwood National Park provide opportunity for close examination of many hardy, perennial herbs, common to northcoast beaches. Near driftline, sea rocket *(Cakile maritima)* grows with fleshy, deeply divided leaves. Sea rocket is a member of the mustard family and bears unusual, lumpy fruit with two triangular flaps near their base. Scattered with sea rocket are two, large, similar-appearing grasses. Only wild rye *(Elymus mollis)* is native to the park. Introduced during sand dune stabilization programs was beach grass *(Ammophila arenaria)*. Vegetation similar to beach grass is common along shores of the Atlantic seaboard and Great Lakes.

Above reach of seasonal high water, beach strawberry *(Fragaria chiloensis)* grows short-stemmed flowers and small, three-parted leaves. During autumn, the five-petalled flowers develop into small, tasty fruit which were gathered by Native Americans. Frequently growing with beach strawberry is beach morning glory *(Calystegia soldanella)*. Unlike domestic morning glory, plants common to the beaches of Redwood National Park seldom climb to great heights. Visitors may identify these colorful plants by their thick, kidney-shaped leaves and purplish flowers.

Yellow sand verbena *(Abronia latifolia)* has rounded, sticky leaves which often collect sand. Flowers of verbena are sweet-scented, yellow and bloom from May to July.

Ice plant *(Carpobrotus chilense)* may be called by a variety of names, including Indian pipe and ghost flower. It has thick, succulent leaves and pink flowers which may remind visitors of cactus or daisies. Nearby, beach evening primrose *(Oenothera cheiranthifolia)* present wilted remains of yellow, four-petalled flowers and a few buds which open at evening. Such primrose is related to fireweed. Also common to beaches of Redwood National Park are golden rod *(Solidago spathulata)* and knotweed *(Polygonum paronychia)*. More than 80 species of golden rod occur throughout the United States. Bright, pyramidal clusters first appear in July and continue until late autumn. Boiled flowers of golden rod yield brilliant, permanent, yellow dye. Knotweed is a low-growing herb with pink flowers. Visitors may be familiar with weedy relatives of knotweed as such plants commonly grow in sidewalk cracks near the park.

MUSHROOMS AND FUNGI

Within Redwood National Park, visitors may examine two of the best growth areas for mushrooms and fungi north of San Francisco. Nearly 570 species of fleshy fungi have been identified by researchers and botanists who study plantlife of the park. Best locations for viewing mushrooms are along margins of Davison Road within Prairie Creek Redwoods State Park and near streamside groves of Jedediah Smith Redwoods State Park.

All plants and vegetation of Redwood National Park are protected. Before collecting mushrooms, visitors should contact personnel of the park administration regarding current policy for such collection. Within Redwood National Park federal lands, visitors may obtain current information in person, or in writing:

Superintendent
Redwood National Park
P.O. Drawer N
Crescent City, California 95531

Telephone: (707) 464-6101

Visitors within California State Park lands may obtain current information in person at the appropriate park office, or by writing:

Area Manager
Prairie Creek Redwoods State Park
Orick, California 95555

Telephone: (707) 488-2171

Area Manager
Del Norte Coast Redwoods State Park
Route 2, Box 286
Crescent City, California 95531

Telephone: (707) 458-3115

Area Manager
Jedediah Smith Redwoods State Park
Route 2, Box 286
Crescent City, California 95531

Telephone: (707) 458-3115

Mushroom collecting has been aptly described by enthusiasts as the most hazardous of sports. Both illness and death may occur from eating toxic mushrooms. Visitors who wish to collect fungi for eating should obtain a suitable reference manual which provides proper guidelines to both mushroom identification and collection. Three suitable reference books recommended for such collection are:

Savory Wild Mushrooms, *by Margaret McKenny and Daniel E. Stuntz. (University of Washington Press, Seattle: 1972).*

Mushrooms of North America, *by Orson K. Miller. (E. P. Dutton and Co., New York: 1972).*

How to Identify Mushrooms (to Genus) Using Only Macroscopic Features, *by David L. Largent. (Mad River Press, Arcata, California: 1973).*

Despite ideal climate conditions which include higher precipitation, abundant humidity, lack of heat and few extensive winter frosts, few mushrooms may be found by visitors to mature redwood forest. Researchers feel that both high calcium soils and presence of fungus-killing agents in redwood forest may limit mushroom growth.

Among visible features of park mushrooms and fungi of interest to visitors are a wide range of shapes and colors. Fungal colors rival those of flowering plants and may range from pure white to pink, red or yellow. Warm colors, including earth tones of orange and reddish brown are most common. Visitors may also view fungi which are blue-gray and black although such colors are rare. Park mushrooms and fungi also grow in a wide variety of shapes. Mushrooms differ from other fungi by having gills on the underside of their caps. Visitors may see within Redwood National Park both classic, disc-shaped mushrooms and cauliflower-like fungi.

Mushrooms may range in odor from fruit or nut-like, to mealy, rancid or chlorine. Odor should not be used, however, to distinguish edible from non-edible species; many toxic mushrooms resemble non-toxic varieties in smell.

Among mushrooms commonly seen within Redwood National Park are those found growing near Gold Bluff beach. Such mushrooms include *Boletus edulis*, with a large, brown to cinnamon-colored cap. Boletus mushrooms are edible and commonly have enlarged, bulb-like bases.

Visitors may also see along the park seacoast poisonous *Amanita muscaria*. Such fungi contain amanitine, an extremely toxic compound, and may be distinguished by their broad, convex or flat caps of yellow, orange, or brilliant red. White gills line the underside of Amanita caps.

Cantharellus cibarius commonly have broad caps and are light to dark yellow in color. The cap may be hairy when young and is often lined at its edge with a recurved border. Wrinkled grooves commonly extend downstem on such mushrooms. Cantharellus is edible.

Near Jedediah Smith Redwoods State Park campground, visitors may see many common species of mushroom and fungi. Most visible are *Pholiota carbonaria*, which commonly grow beside campsite fireplaces on decomposed firewood, and shaggy-maned *Coprinus comatus.* Coprinus mushrooms are edible and grow woolly scales which give them their hairy appearance. The cap of such fungi are commonly three inches *(7.6 cm)* tall and are egg-shaped when young.

A poisonous relative of Coprinus comatus, *Coprinus atramentarius*, grow brownish-gray, scaly caps which are often grooved near the edge. Such mushrooms are frequently less than four inches *(10.2 cm)* tall and have narrow, bell-shaped caps.

Another common mushroom visible to park visitors is *Lycoperdon perlatum*, which has a thick, pear-shaped outer skin covered with small, round, pointed spines. Such spines may break and leave round, dull to light tan spots. Nearby, *Agaricus placomyces* have a distinctive, almost creosote-like smell. When such mushrooms first appear, they range in color from light to dark pink. After spores mature, however, they become nearly chocolate-brown.

Visitors may see mushroom and fungi throughout all seasons of the year. Peak periods of growth, however, occur from late August to mid-December. During this time, in early November, members of the *California Native Plant Society* conduct a mushroom walk. Visitors wishing information regarding mushroom walks conducted by the society may contact:

> *Secretary*
> *California Native Plant Society*
> *525 Herrick Avenue*
> *Eureka, California 95501*
>
> *Telephone: (707) 443-7404*

Many anglers visit Redwood National Park because of the fine fishing available within its boundaries. Throughout the year, but especially in autumn and spring, large runs of steelhead, silver salmon and king salmon enter park streams and rivers, providing exciting fishing to visitors. On park seacoasts, rock fishermen may catch sea trout, skulpin, black rockfish, ling cod, cabezon and several species of surf perch. Visitors on nearby sandy beaches can net surf smelt, night fish and candlefish. Anglers with boats may fish offshore for silver and king salmon during late spring and summer.

All fishing within Redwood National Park must conform to regulations published annually by the California Department of Fish and Game. Regulations require anglers within both federal and state park waters to hold a valid California sportsfishing license. Such licenses may be either resident or non-resident, 10-day special or full-season, and are obtained from retail shops that deal in fishing or sports equipment. Residency within the State of California for fishing license purposes requires a minimum of six months state occupancy.

Regulations governing fishing of park waters are subject to change, and visitors should acquaint themselves with current requirements. Annual publications of the California Department of Fish and Game are available from licensing agents near the park, or may be obtained by writing:

Director
California Department of Fish and Game
1416 Ninth Street
Sacramento, California 95814

Trout. Anglers in park waters may catch California cutthroat and rainbow trout, as well as immature king and silver salmon. Cutthroat trout are found in most seacoast lagoons, streams and rivers from southern Oregon to mid-northern California. Most cutthroat caught within park waters are sea-run and may occasionally reach lengths as great as 18 inches *(46 cm)*. Because some fish spend only a few months at sea, however, those longer than 11 inches *(28 cm)* are considered large. California cutthroat trout enter park streams to spawn during late autumn and early winter. They are most abundant at these times in lower Smith and Klamath rivers and near the mouth of Redwood Creek.

Visitors to the park may also catch juvenile, or resident, cutthroat. Such fish have not yet migrated to sea, are immature sexually and seldom reach lengths greater than 10 inches *(25 cm)*. Fishermen may identify both sea-run and resident California cutthroat by their distinctive red or orange dash behind the mouth and tiny teeth behind the base of the tongue.

Native, or resident, rainbow trout are occasionally caught in small streams and headwater tributaries of larger waterways. Such fish are seldom longer than eight inches *(20.3 cm)*, but may contain eggs, or spawn, and be several years or more old. Resident rainbow grow more slowly than fish that migrate to sea and may be identified by their colorful side markings, missing basal teeth on the tongue and lack the cutthroat dash behind the mouth.

Young silver and king salmon are frequently caught by fly and spinner fishermen. Such fish are small, usually less than seven inches *(17.8 cm)* long, and have not yet migrated to sea. Silver salmon fingerlings and juveniles may be identified by their small, black spots dotting the back, dorsal fin and upper half of the tail fin. Young king salmon, by comparison, have large black spots throughout their back, dorsal fin and entire tail.

Salmon and Steelhead. Most important to park fishermen are king and silver salmon, and steelhead. All three types of fish reach great size, fight admirably when caught and provide excellent eating. Best opportunities for catching steelhead and salmon occur in tidal areas of major park rivers and streams.

Klamath and Smith rivers during autumn are excellent fishing grounds, but steelhead sometimes may be caught far inland. Salmon also frequent coast waters off park shores from May through September. Two species of·sea-run rainbow trout, or steelhead, occur naturally in park streams. Most spawning occurs during autumn, when mature adult fish enter fresh water and travel upriver to shallow tributary streams. A few fish also move upstream during spring, remain in deep holes during summer and spawn in August. Autumn and winter-run steelhead may average nearly eight pounds *(3.6 kg)* and reach lengths greater than 20 inches *(51 cm)*.

Smaller steelhead, locally referred to as half-pounders, occasionally may be caught within streams and rivers to Redwood National Park. Such fish seem nearly restricted to northern California, resemble large, adult steelhead and are sexually immature. Most half-pounders enter the sea after one or two years in fresh water streams, then return to feed on spawn of salmon and mature steelhead, washed from gravel beds upstream after only a few months at sea. Most are 11 *(29 cm)* to 15 inches *(38 cm)* long, and a few may weigh 18 ounces *(510 g)* or more. Half-pounders appear in park streams during August and run through October. Best fishing for half-pounders takes place in Klamath River, although a few fish are caught annually in Redwood Creek.

Fishermen may distinguish both half-pounders and mature steelhead from large cutthroat trout by their lack of a dash behind the mouth and missing teeth near the base of the tongue. Many steelhead survive autumn spawning and return downstream to the sea. Such fish are called run-backs and may return in successive years to spawn within the park. Run-back steelhead often have less tasty meat than fish fresh from salt water but provide lively action to anglers.

Silver salmon, like steelhead, spawn in many streams and tributaries of Redwood National Park. Best fishing for silver salmon occurs from November to January, when anglers may find salmon in tidal areas of Smith and Klamath rivers and many smaller waterways. Silver salmon usually spawn in very shallow creeks, often in water only two *(5 cm)* to four inches *(10 cm)* deep.

During spawning, female silver salmon create nests of river gravel by washing the stream bottom with their tails. A few eggs are released, fertilized by male milt, then lightly covered with sand. Repeated egg laying, fertilization and covering continues until all are released. Both males and females die within a short time. If muddy water, silting or sudden drops in temperature do not cause death within the egg, young fish, or alevins, hatch in a few weeks. Such fish feed for a time on food from their yolk sac, then begin foraging for microscopic plants and animals. Most fish develop in fresh water for one season before migrating to sea. During this time, alevins grow to fingerlings, then to trout-sized fish. During downstream migration, yearling silver salmon are large enough to be caught by fishermen, but late season openings prevent all but minor catches.

After one to two seasons at sea, silver salmon mature sexually and complete their life cycles. Many adults reach weights of nine pounds *(4.1 kg)*, but smaller fish, known as chubs or jacks, may weigh only two pounds *(.9 kg)*. Such fish are sexually mature but do not remain at sea as long as full-sized salmon.

Anglers may most easily identify mature silver salmon by their distinctive white-gummed mouth and small, black spots which extend only halfway down the tail fin.

King salmon enter larger park rivers and streams during autumn, although occasional fish migrate upriver during spring, survive low summer water in deep holes, and spawn during autumn. Many king salmon enter Klamath River during midsummer, beginning spawning runs which extend nearly until October. Such early fish result from the great length of the river; first fish caught must travel the greatest distance upriver to spawn. Other park streams, including Smith River, Redwood Creek, and Prairie Creek have later, smaller runs of king salmon.

Spawning of mature king salmon usually occurs from October to January in main streams and larger tributary waterways. Like silver salmon, runs may contain smaller jack or chub salmon. Such fish often return to fresh water after a single season in the ocean and may weigh only four pounds *(1.8 kg)*. Many adult kings weigh more than 10 pounds *(4.5 kg)*, and exceptionally large fish weigh as much as 40 pounds *(18.2 kg)*.

Because of their great size, king salmon pose the most exciting fishing available to park anglers.

FISHING PARK STREAMS AND LAGOONS

Freshwater Lagoon. The largest water body within Redwood National Park is Freshwater Lagoon, located 2.5 miles *(4 km)* west of the Orick gateway on U.S. Highway 101. Freshwater Lagoon contains little salt and overflows to the sea only through a culvert beneath the highway at its north end. It receives frequent plantings of hatchery trout, is easily reached and offers convenient fishing. Many anglers find boats effective for fishing lagoon waters, but shore casters also may be successful along U.S. Highway 101 spit.

Fishermen attempting first catches in Freshwater Lagoon should troll slowly near the shore. In such areas, roiling of water by wave action stirs food from the bottom and attracts fish. Many anglers have found artificial lures, including flatfish, wob-L-rites and spinners, best bait for lagoon fishing. Still-fishing with worms is also effective following storms.

Big and Stone Lagoons. A few miles south of Redwood National Park boundaries, two briny, seaside lagoons provide fishing to park visitors. Approximately 2.2 miles *(3.5 km)* south on U.S. Highway 101 is Stone Lagoon, while 2.9 miles *(4.7 km)* further lies Big Lagoon. Both are easily accessible by automobile, provide boat ramp facilities and offer excellent fishing. The sand spits dividing Big and Stone lagoons from waters of the Pacific Ocean are part of Dry Lagoon State Park. A day-use facility is located 3.7 miles *(6.0 km)* south of Redwood National Park between the two lagoons.

Because both Big and Stone lagoons contain brine, a mixture of salt and fresh water, numerous marine fish, including smelt, silverside perch, herring and starry flounder may be occasionally caught by fishermen. Good-sized rainbow and cutthroat trout are common, some as large as two pounds *(.9 kg)*. During spring and autumn some steelhead and silver salmon pass through lagoon waters to spawn in nearby creeks.

During winter, rainstorms cause many park streams to become muddy or otherwise unfishable, but visitors may often fish clear water in Big and Stone lagoons. Anglers who plan boating in lagoon waters, however, should keep a close watch to sea. Frequent, gusty winds caused by Pacific Ocean storms may present hazardous conditions to small craft.

Redwood Creek. Near the Orick gateway, visitors to Redwood National Park may fish Redwood Creek, the largest creek flowing within park boundaries. Headwatered nearly 50 miles *(80 km)* northeast of the park, Redwood Creek flows northwest before entering the park approximately 9.7 miles *(15.6 km)* southeast of Orick. Except for a short portion near Orick, the remainder of the stream flows within Redwood National Park.

Siltation in Redwood Creek during recent years has greatly increased because of forestry and mining efforts outside park boundaries, but is also due to devastating floods in 1955 and 1964. Siltation has filled deep pools and deposited large amounts of fine sediment in riffles, making the stream increasingly less suitable for spawning and growth of salmon and steelhead. California cutthroat trout numbers have also declined during recent years.

Fishing in Redwood Creek may be good, however. The waterway frequently produces very large king and silver salmon, as well as fine steelhead and cutthroat trout. Resident fish which have not yet migrated to sea may also be caught in the stream.

Near its mouth, Redwood Creek also has large runs of euchalon, or candlefish. These silvery, sea-run smelt are related to salmon, and most spawn in fresh water. Candlefish are usually taken by dipping ocean waves with A-frame nets near the stream mouth, early in the year. When dried, such fish are very oily and were used by early settlers for light. A string wick was passed through the body, allowing the fish to gradually yield its oil to the flame. Candlefish provide enjoyable eating when cooked so that excess oil may be lost.

Other species of fish, including sculpin, Humboldt sucker, stickleback and sea-run lamprey, or eel, occur in Redwood Creek but are of little value to fishermen. Lampreys may be seen spawning during spring in riffles of the creek and are caught by local Native Americans who smoke or roast their excellent meat.

Fishermen should carefully observe special limits commonly in effect for Redwood Creek. Portions of the stream below U.S. Highway 101 bridge at Orick are open to fishing year-round, but anglers may only keep three salmon, steelhead or trout. Northeast from the highway bridge, upstream, two miles *(3.2 km)* above its confluence with Prairie Creek, the stream is open to fishing only from November 16 through the Friday preceding Memorial Day. Three fish may be taken during that period. Upstream from the special regulation areas, normal North Coast District season and take limits apply. Special regulations may change from season to season, and visitors should carefully comply.

Prairie Creek. Prairie Creek flows into Redwood Creek one mile *(1.6 km)* northeast of the Orick gateway, near the junction of U.S. Highway 101 and Bald Hills Road. Except for a short distance near its mouth, Prairie Creek flows entirely within park boundaries and remains clear and fishable throughout its special season from October 1 through the Friday preceding Memorial Day. The stream is closed to fishing throughout the rest of the year. Anglers should carefully check current regulations prior to fishing waters of Prairie Creek.

Steelhead, silver salmon, king salmon and California cutthroat trout spawn in Prairie Creek. Fishermen willing to hike to less accessible waters, including those of Brown and Godwood creeks, may catch cutthroat trout as large as 15 inches *(38 cm)*. Best catches result when anglers use dry flies, floating line, and short, pliable rods. Such poles may be easily maneuvered through banks clogged with brush. Bait fishing with worms has also proven effective in Prairie Creek, especially in early morning and evening hours. At such times, fish feed on insects and grubs washed into the stream.

Espa Lagoon. Espa Lagoon, or Barnes Pond, is located .1 mile *(.2 km)* east of Gold Bluff beach on Davison Road. The lagoon is best reached by turning west on Davison Road, 2.6 miles *(4.2 km)* from the Orick gateway information center northeast on U.S. Highway 101. Davison Road is maintained by

Humboldt County and is subject to special vehicle restrictions. No trailers, campers or recreational vehicles exceeding widths of seven feet *(2.1 m)* or lengths greater than 20 feet *(6.1 m)*, either single or in combination, are allowed.

Espa Lagoon is quite small but frequently receives plantings of cutthroat trout and other species. Margins of the lagoon are marshy, and best results occur when anglers use bait or artificial lures equipped with weed protectors.

Prairie Creek Fish Hatchery. One mile *(1.6 km)* north on U.S. Highway 101, from its junction with Davison Road, visitors to the park may visit Prairie Creek Fish Hatchery, a facility operated by Humboldt County. The hatchery was built more than 30 years ago and rears salmon and trout for stocking northcoast streams and lagoons. Fishermen may enjoy seeing fish in many stages of development, from egg to release size, 10 inches *(25 cm)* or more long.

Klamath River. Located 22.3 miles *(36 km)* from the Orick gateway, north on U.S. Highway 101, Klamath River is the largest river passing through Redwood National Park. Headwatered in high mountains of Oregon, the river is not typical of redwood streams and contains many species of fish not found elsewhere in the region. Among fish available to Klamath River anglers are steelhead, silver and king salmon, euchalon, California cutthroat trout, green sturgeon, yellow perch, and Klamath River speckled dace. Some species occur only as strays in the lower river and have been carried downstream by high water.

Best known for excellent salmon and steelhead fishing, Klamath River receives first spawning runs in mid-summer, when half-pounders begin upriver migrations. Many fish may be taken on artificial flies, but they will also strike a wide variety of trout lures and bait. By mid-July, king salmon enter the river to spawn, followed by large steelhead in September. Salmon and steelhead runs continue until spring, and anglers may catch a wide variety of hard-fighting, highly tasty fish throughout the length of the river.

The intertidal estuary near Klamath River mouth provides best fishing near the park. Casters from shore join crowded boats to hook fish entering the stream from the Pacific Ocean. Some fishermen anchor just inside the mouth of the river, forming bank to bank rows, several boats deep. Personnel of the U.S. Coast Guard must frequently caution such fishermen, however, as changing tides and strong currents promote hazardous conditions.

Anglers may fish Klamath River waters year-round. Downstream from U.S. Highway 101 bridge, daily limits are three trout or salmon in combination. Above the highway bridge, three trout or salmon in combination may be taken, except during the general trout season, when the limit increases to 10 trout or salmon in combination, but not more than 10 pounds *(4.5 kg)* total, plus one fish. All fishermen should consult current regulations prior to fishing Klamath River waters.

Salmon and steelhead fishermen may wish to rent or lease boats for fishing lower Klamath River. Many private firms located near the river mouth provide such service to park visitors. Reservations, except during peak periods, are unnecessary.

Klamath River also has large runs of candlefish. Such fish first enter the river in February, have peak runs during March and April, and continue in smaller numbers until May. Best method of fishing for candlefish is by dip-netting near Klamath Glen, 3.1 miles *(5 km)* east along the north bank of Klamath River, from U.S. Highway 101 bridge. Porpoises, seals and sea lions sometimes follow the run far upstream, adding noisy excitement to the fishing.

California cutthroat trout may be taken in the lower river throughout the year. Tidal waters near Requa sometimes provide good fishing during February and March, when sea-run cutthroat which have spawned return to the ocean.

Green sturgeon are common in deep holes along lower Klamath River during late summer and early autumn. Such fish will take kidney and earthworm baits readily and pose exciting fishing to anglers with sturdy tackle. Sturgeon sometimes reach lengths greater than seven feet *(2.1 m)*.

Lagoon Creek Fishing Access. Approximately 5.5 miles *(8.8 km)* from Klamath, north on U.S. Highway 101, visitors to Redwood National Park may fish waters of Lagoon Creek. A day-use picnic facility adjoins the highway, providing parking near the lagoon. Lagoon Creek is a log pond remaining from sawmill activities in the area during recent years, and contains California cutthroat trout. Anglers using bait, artificial lures and weighted flies will have best results, especially near its ocean outlet northwest of the picnic grounds.

Mill Creek. Approximately 8.5 miles *(13.7 km)* from Lagoon Creek, north on U.S. Highway 101, anglers approach Del Norte Coast Redwoods State Park campground, situated on Mill

Creek. The waters of Mill Creek provide early season fishing for cutthroat and rainbow trout. Flies and artificial lures have proven effective, as have artificial lures which mimic roe or eggs. Fishermen may also approach Mill Creek by following Elk Valley Road, located .2 mile (.3 km) south of the Crescent City gateway on U.S. Highway 101. Elk Valley Road travels eastward to the boundary of Jedediah Smith Redwoods State Park, where it junctions with Howland Hill Road. Howland Hill Road is narrow, but visitors with small vehicles may follow it northeast 4.3 miles (6.9 km) to a bridge over Mill Creek.

During autumn, visitors to Mill Creek may view spawning king salmon by cautiously approaching the water edge. Best time to see such activity is during late October, when waters are clear and low.

Mill Creek is open to fishing year-round. Except during the general trout season from the Saturday preceding Memorial Day through November 15, the limit is three fish. During general trout season, limits increase to 10 trout or salmon, but not more than 10 pounds (4.5 kg) total, plus one fish.

Smith River. Waters of Smith River pass briefly through park boundaries at Jedediah Smith Redwoods State Park. Second largest among park rivers, it is perhaps the most scenic. Rocky, upstream slopes help the river to clear rapidly following heavy rains, allow little siltation of riffles, and promote good summertime flow of cool water.

Smith River is widely known for California cutthroat, large king and silver salmon, and numerous steelhead. The five miles (8 km) of waterway flowing through the park produce many large fish each year. Most are caught from autumn to midwinter by anglers using flies which initiate young smolt or eggs. In murky water, flashers and attracters have been used successfully for catching steelhead and salmon. Artificial lures are effective during low water, when large fish settle into deep holes downstream from obstacles.

Many steelhead caught in Smith River are taken upon return to the ocean following spawning. While run-back fish tend to be weakened by spawning and upstream migration, they are often full of fight. Outside park boundaries, near the mouth of the Smith, many such fish are caught by anglers.

FISHING PARK BEACHES AND SEACOAST

Redwood National Park borders waters of the Pacific Ocean for nearly its entire length. Fishermen may choose from rugged, rocky coastlines or broad, sandy beaches. In nearby gateway communities, anglers may launch or charter boats for deep sea fishing. Many species, including king and silver salmon, red-tailed perch, ling cod, cabezon, black rockfish and surf fish, or smelt, may be caught. Equipment may range from heavy ocean rods and reels to A-frame nets or bare hands. Where roads provide access, entire families may join the excitement of ocean fishing.

Sandy Beaches. Along open, sandy beaches such as those found near the mouth of Redwood Creek, Gold Bluff beach or False Klamath Cove, visitors may fish for surf perch, night fish and surf fish. Red-tailed perch are most commonly caught by visitors on hook and line. Best bait for surf-casting northcoast waters are tube and mud worms, collected in margins of Humboldt Bay, 38.5 miles *(62 km)* south of park boundaries. Such worms are either raked from pilings or dug from bay mud prior to fishing. Anglers may also use earthworms, sand crabs, clams or shrimp with success.

Fishing equipped with A-frame nets of small mesh may dip ocean waves for surf fish, or smelt. Such fish are silvery, about six inches *(15.2 cm)* long, and when cooked soon after catch provide excellent eating. Related smelt, locally called night fish, are smaller. Night fish may be caught during evening hours in early spring in much the same manner as surf fish. Both fish follow ocean waves high on sloping beaches to spawn. When heavy runs occur, both night and day fish may be stranded by retreating waters. At such times, visitors may pick them from the water by hand.

Rocky Seacoast. Rocky areas provide good locations for fishermen equipped with casting rods and heavy line. A wide variety of rock fish may be caught, including sea trout, perch, cabezon and ling cod. Best areas for rock fishing occur south of Crescent Bay, 3.5 miles *(5.6 km)* south of the Crescent City

gateway. Fishermen may also have good luck on rocky promontories of Coastal Drive, a highway loop which departs U.S.
Highway 101 one mile *(1.6 km)* south of Klamath River
highway bridge. It rejoins the highway 4.6 miles *(7.4 km)*
south.

Bait used for rock fishing in park waters includes tube and
mud worms, clams, mussels, shrimp and cut fish. Visitors
intending such fishing should include an adequate sunburn
preventative; sunlight filtering through salt air is deceptively
strong, even on partially overcast days. Windbreakers or warm
jackets may also be necessary as rocky areas suitable for fishing
may be exposed to strong, cool winds.

Deep Sea Fishing. Offshore waters of Redwood National Park
provide excellent opportunities for salmon fishing. As summer
winds steady from the northwest each spring, upwelling of
deep, nutrient-rich waters begins near the coast. Small fish
enter upwelling water to eat microscopic plankton and are
followed, in turn, by feeding salmon. Throughout the summer,
salmon remain offshore and are frequently caught in great
numbers.

Best opportunities for anglers seeking deep sea fishing near Redwood National Park occur at Eureka, 40 miles *(64 km)* south on U.S. Highway 101, Trinidad, 17 miles *(27 km)* south on U.S. Highway 101, and at the Crescent City gateway. Launching facilities exist at each community, and visitors may rent or charter boats for fishing.

Most successful equipment for ocean salmon fishing include heavy rods and line, anchovy bait with double harness hooks, double swivels, bright flashers, and heavy drop-off sinkers. Ocean salmon may reach weights as heavy as 45 pounds *(20.4 kg)*, lengths greater than four feet *(1.2 m)* and provide exciting fishing even to experienced anglers.

Fishermen seeking king and silver salmon in ocean waters usually troll a mile or more offshore. Because seacoast fogs are common during summer, such fishing requires local knowledge, a good compass, and adequate planning. Entry into Humboldt Bay from the ocean may become extremely hazardous under adverse wind and tide conditions, even on relatively calm summer days. Always file a float plan with the Coast Guard before attempting such fishing.

HIKING AND WATERCRAFT TRAILS

Redwood National Park offers a gentle wilderness to back-country travelers. Over 100 miles *(160.9 km)* of prepared hiking trails and routes link campgrounds and day-use facilities with areas of scenic interest. Three major rivers provide pathways to watercraft users and fishermen. Near the seacoast, park visitors may explore nearly 40 miles *(64.4 km)* of rugged, scenic coastline on paths which lead from rocky promontories to sandy beaches.

Most trails within the park are old, heavily used, and well maintained. When compared with hiking routes common to more rugged alpine areas, such trails may resemble backyard or garden paths. Wooden bridges cross most creeks and rivers, and seldom must hikers ford waterways on foot. Instead of vistas of grandeur common to other parks, visitors tend to closely examine features close at hand while shadowed by the immensity of coast redwood forest. Perspective returns to tiny mosses, ferns, lichens and fungi.

Use Areas. Visitors planning backcountry use within Redwood National Park should obtain current information regarding trail and campsite conditions from personnel of the National Park Service. Because the park was established only recently, few facilities have been developed on federal lands, and most campsites and picnic areas are administered by personnel of the California State Department of Parks and Recreation. Two backpacking areas are recognized by the National Park Service as campsites: Redwood Creek corridor and Nickel Creek.

Pets. No pets are allowed on trails. In addition, dogs must remain on a lead less than six feet *(1.8 m)* while in campground areas. Vicious or unusually noisy animals will not be allowed within the park. At night, all pets must be kept within enclosed vehicles or tents. Personnel of the park administration suggest that visitors intending overnight use board their animals at kennels available in nearby gateway cities. Pets within state park campsites require visitor fees of $.50 per pet, per night.

Fire Permits. No fire permits are required for camping in designated campsites. Visitors intending backpack use of national park areas should obtain a free fire permit at either Orick or Crescent City gateway. Visitors are cautioned that all plantlife is protected within the park. Only driftwood found on beaches or river gravel bars may be collected for burning. Self-contained backpack stoves, such as those manufactured by *Optimus* and *Primus*, are more suitable for cooking.

Litter. The golden rule of backpacking is that all garbage carried in, comes out. Unsightly litter habits should not spoil the wilderness for other visitors. Personnel of both national and state park administrations recommend the use of freeze-dried foods instead of canned or bottled stores. Such materials are packaged in foil and plastic containers which should be properly disposed of in litter receptacles.

Camping. All park overnight facilities except Nickel Creek Campground are operated by California State Department of Parks and Recreation. The federal Golden Eagle passport is not valid in these campgrounds, and visitors must pay current California rates outlined in Gateways and Facilities. Reservations must be obtained in person through Ticketron, or by writing:

> *Ticketron*
> *5151 W. Imperial Highway*
> *Inglewood, California 90304*

Backpacking. Visitors who wish to extend their journey to northern California with rugged backcountry travel may do so by utilizing trail systems of Six Rivers National Forest, located east of the park. Six Rivers provides 25 hiking trails suitable for backpackers. Visitors seeking additional information should write:

Administrator
Six Rivers National Forest
710 E. Street
Eureka, California 95501

Telephone: (707) 442-1721

Climate and Weather. Visitors intending backcountry use of Redwood National Park should expect both sunny and warm, as well as rainy and cool, weather. Best weather in the park occurs during spring and autumn, with foggy summers and rainy winters. Those intending overnight camping during winter should carry tents and clothing suitable for extended downpour. Areas near the coast may be cool, while inland portions often experience clear weather throughout the summer. Visitors seeking additional information regarding climate should read the chapter on Climate and Weather.

Fishing. A valid California sportsfishing license is required for angling both national and state park waters. Licenses may be obtained from sports shops and many retail merchants near the park. Either a 10-day special or full season license, resident or non-resident is suitable. Additional information regarding rules and regulations for fishing park waters may be obtained by reading the chapter on Fishing.

Wildlife Hazard. Visitors traveling trails near Prairie Creek Redwoods State Park should carefully avoid close approach to Roosevelt elk. Such animals may appear docile and tame, but are wild creatures. If hikers should encounter elk while walking paths or beaches of the park, give the animals a wide berth. Do not separate a cow elk from her calf, nor make sudden moves near bulls during autumn rut.

Rattlesnakes may be encountered rarely during summer near inland rivers and grassy meadows. Visitors to such areas should be careful at all times to watch their footing.

Skunks and porcupines may prove a nuisance to some

visitors. Neither animal is dangerous unless provoked, however. Skunks may be distinguished by their distinctive black and white coloration. Both spotted and striped skunks occur throughout the park. Porcupines are most commonly found eating the tender bark of willow and alder in streamside forests. They may be quite large, frequently reaching 15 pounds *(6.8 kg)* or more. Porcupines do not throw quills, and must be touched to inflict injury.

Hikers are requested to report any incident of animal bite or unusual behavior to personnel of either the State or National park administration.

Sun Protection. Seacoast areas of the park frequently receive strong, direct sunlight in combination with salt air. Even on overcast days, sunburn is likely if visitors do not take ample protective measures. Hikers and watercraft operators near such areas should carefully apply a protective lotion, such as *Sea-n-Ski* or *Coppertone.*

HIKING PARK TRAILS

The 20 trails of EXPLORING REDWOOD NATIONAL PARK are ordered both by difficulty and area within the park. Trails range from easy walks over level ground to difficult treks over uneven terrain. Hikers may easily obtain information regarding the route followed by studying the capsule information describing the hike. Points of interest, length of hike, necessary equipment and necessary maps help provide information of use to visitors.

Because trail conditions may vary from season to season, visitors should inquire as to current status of the hikes described. Such inquiries may be directed to personnel of the California State Park administration, located in each state park.

FLOATING PARK RIVERS

Three major waterways provide watercraft trails to park visitors: Smith and Klamath rivers and Redwood Creek. Park streams may often be cloudy with transported sediment. Trails described range from gentle, one-day floats to whitewater journeys which challenge the most experienced enthusiast.

River Ratings. Most rivers within the United States are rated for navigability on a scale from Class I to Class VI. Class ratings may be applied both to rivers in general and to specific rapids. Such ratings provide guidelines to difficulty.

Class ratings are only approximations. Degrees of difficulty may be largely dependent on skill and experience. Class III rapids may be equally dangerous as Class V water to one without proper equipment or training.

River ratings, and their meanings, are:

Class I: *Easy, flat-moving water.*

Class II: *Moving water with strong currents, riffles and waves. Requires general caution.*

Class III: *Difficult, technical and precise maneuvering required.*

Class IV: *Very difficult with strong currents, waves and obstacles. Highly technical maneuvering required.*

Class V: *Extreme difficulty. Class IV water with rescue and recovery generally impossible.*

Class VI: *Absolute limit of navigability. Should be attempted only be teams of experts under favorable conditions, including local knowledge.*

TRIP ONE

LADY BIRD JOHNSON GROVE WALK

Begins: Johnson Grove parking access, mile 2.8 (km 4.5),
Bald Hills Road.
Ends: Johnson Grove parking access, mile 2.8 (km 4.5),
Bald Hills Road.
Approximate Distance: .3 mile (.5 km) round trip.
Approximate Hiking Time: 1 hour.
Difficulty: Easy.
Maps: None required.

Remarks: An ideal walk for those with limited time.
Redwood National Park was dedicated at Lady
Bird Johnson Grove on November 25, 1968.

Visitors wishing to view the dedication site for Redwood National Park should follow U.S. Highway 101 1.4 miles *(2.3 km)* north of the Orick gateway to Bald Hills Road. Because Bald Hills Road is winding, steep and narrow, visitors towing trailers should leave their trailers at the access parking area, located .6 mile *(1 km)* from the turnoff. Unencumbered vehicles should then proceed to the starting point, mile 2.8 *(km 4.5)*, Bald Hills Road. A parking access and pedestrian bridge spanning Bald Hills Road leads to Lady Bird Johnson Grove.

Visitors may notice both stumps and mature trees near trailhead. Coast redwood forests near the grove were thinned by private owners prior to establishment of the park in 1968. Because

thinning increased light to the forest floor, several other species of trees, including Douglas fir, have sprouted nearby. Douglas fir may be distinguished by its circular, radiating needles.

Visitors should travel north along the trail, observing coast redwood hollowed by a combination of repeated forest fires and rot. The cambium growth layers of such trees remain undamaged, and many live to great age. About .1 mile *(.2 km)* from trailhead, visitors may examine an interpretive plaque describing the dedication ceremony of November 25, 1968. Mrs. Johnson, accompanied by her husband and President Richard M. Nixon, unveiled the cairn with help of dignitaries of both National Park Service and State of California. The ceremony crowned efforts to establish a

Redwood National Park lasting nearly 100 years.

Near the dedication site, visitors may also overlook a forested area cut prior to Congressional approval of the act. Interpretive plaques describe several common techniques used in logging. Visitors may return to the parking access on a short, self-guided nature trail describing many features of coast redwood forest.

TRIP TWO

REDWOOD CREEK HIKE

Begins: Redwood Creek parking access,
    mile .8 (km 1.2), Bald Hills Road.
Ends: Redwood Creek parking access,
    mile .8 (km 1.2), Bald Hills Road.
Approximate Distance: 16 miles (25.7 km) round trip.
Approximate Hiking Time: 2 days.
Difficulty: Easy to moderate.
Special Equipment: Hikers overnight on gravel bars of
    Redwood Creek near Tall Trees
    Grove.
Maps: U.S.G.S. Topographic Sheets, Orick and
    Rodgers Peak, Calif. N4115-W12400/7.5
    and N4107.5-W12400/7.5
    1966.

Remarks: Hikers follow Redwood Creek to Tall Trees
    Grove, site of the tallest known coast red-
    wood. Several creek fordings are necessary,
    and hikers should outfit with hiking boots
    suitable for several wettings. Because of
    probable route changes during summer
    visitor season 1974 and 1975, hikers should
    contact personnel at Orick gateway for
    current trail information.

Redwood Creek Hike provides the only true backpacking route available to park visitors. Hikers reach the starting point by following U.S. Highway 101 north from the Orick gateway 1.4 miles (2.3 km) to Bald Hills Road. Travel east along the road .8 mile (1.2 km) to a parking access at trailhead.

From the starting point, hikers should follow the trail southeast .6 mile (1 km) to a grove of Sitka spruce and the bank of Redwood Creek. The trail then turns south, following a streamside meadow to the first fording point. High water during winter rainy periods may make the route impassible. Hikers should always ford park streams in suitable footgear. If a traveler does not wish to wet hiking boots during such crossings, other footwear, such as tennis shoes, should be carried. Redwood Creek may,

at times, be very deep and hazardous. Hikers should be particularly careful to avoid "black rocks," slippery with moss.

From the fording point, the trail follows the west bank of Redwood Creek upstream. During summer low water, hikers may follow gravel bars nearly to Tall Trees Grove. Enroute, travelers may easily see lands forested by private timber owners. Such cutting has proceeded to park boundaries in many areas.

At 7.5 miles (12.1 km) from trailhead, hikers find themselves opposite Tall Trees Grove, site of the Howard A. Libby, or Tall Tree. Tall Tree is the highest known coast redwood, stretching 367.8 feet (112.1 m). It was discovered in 1963 by a party of National Geographic Society scientists led by Dr. Paul Zahl.

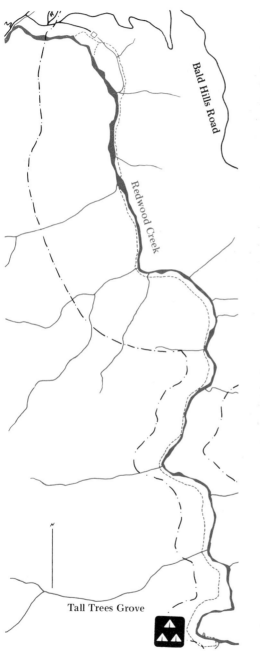

Bald Hills Road

Redwood Creek

Tall Trees Grove

Hikers should overnight on the river gravel bar. No backpacking camping within forest areas is permitted. When camping, use only river driftwood for fire, not down wood. Carry-in backpacking stoves are much preferred.

Return to the starting point the next day by following the outbound route.

TRIP THREE

REVELATION TRAIL FOR THE BLIND

Begins: Elk Prairie Campground, Prairie Creek
        Redwoods State Park.
Ends: Elk Prairie Campground, Prairie Creek
        Redwoods State Park.
Approximate Distance: .2 mile (.3 km).
Approximate Hiking Time: 30 minutes.
Difficulty: Easy.
Special Equipment: None normally required.
        Blind visitors may obtain
        a special braille guide to
        the trail from personnel
        of the park administration.
Maps: None required.

Remarks: Revelation Trail is a unique
interpretive nature trail designed
for use both by sighted and non-
sighted visitors. The trail explores
coast redwood forest through the
senses of touch, hearing and smell.

To most park visitors, coast redwood forest such as the streamside
groves located at Prairie Creek
Redwoods State Park are remarkable because of their spectacular
scenery. To those without sight,
however, the transition from met-
ropolitan to wilderness is more
subtle. A gradual awareness of
wildlife sounds, clean air and soft
forest floor underfoot replaces the
harshness of city life.

Revelation Trail was built in
1971 by personnel of the park
administration with the aid of
funding supplied by members of
Save-The-Redwoods League. The
trail begins 200 yards *(183 m)*
southwest of park headquarters
along the campground road.

From the parking area the path
follows a circular pathway past a
series of interpretive plaques describing natural features of coast
redwood forest. Included are redwood, tanoak, western hemlock,
the forest floor, California laurel
and a rest area near Prairie Creek.

The braille text used by blind
persons while walking Revelation
Trail differs only slightly from
information contained on the
plaques at trailside. It was tran-
scribed by Mrs. Sharon Christian,
a teacher of the visually handi-
capped who lives in Eureka.
Sighted visitors may enjoy the
following extract of the braille
trail guide.

*Approaching Text seven find
low shrubs, log, little plants directly across trail two paces. Read
Text Seven. The Forest Floor.
Gently feel the living plants, the
larger limbs, twigs and leaves on
the forest floor. Push your fin-
gers down into the layer of* Forest

Duff. *Duff, as distinguished from dirt, is fallen material being decayed by countless kinds and numbers of microscopic organisms.*

Below this surface layer, the pieces are smaller. Deep down is a mixture of rich, decayed material. These layers provide the forest with resistance to erosion, protection from heat and drying and a source of food and minerals. Duff has a sharp, clean smell which often dominates other forest odors. Take a whiff and remember the smell.

TRIP FOUR

ELK PRAIRIE WALK

Begins: Elk Prairie Campground, Prairie Creek Redwoods State Park.
Ends: Elk Prairie Campground, Prairie Creek Redwoods State Park.
Approximate Distance: 2.3 miles (3.7 km).
Approximate Hiking Time: 2 hours.
Difficulty: Easy.
Special Equipment: None normally required. Binoculars or a camera may prove helpful for observing wildlife.
Maps: U.S.G.S. Topographic Sheet, Orick, Calif. N4115-W12400/7.5 1966.

Remarks: Elk Prairie Walk provides campground visitors excellent views of Roosevelt elk, streamside forest and meadows. Hikers should not approach elk closely, however, as they are wild animals. If elk are encountered on the trail while hiking, back away slowly. All hikers should carefully read the section on wildlife hazard.

The walk begins between campsites 67 and 69. Hikers should follow the trail parelleling Prairie Creek southwest, in and out of mixed-conifer forest. Side trails nearby are paths used by park elk. Near the south end of the meadow the trail passes several maintenance buildings, then turns eastward to cross U.S. Highway 101.

Elk Prairie meadow is not a natural feature. Its land was cleared by early settlers who raised hay in the opening. Near its margins, smaller trees may be seen slowly closing the opening, a process called encroachment.

After crossing U.S. Highway 101, hikers should follow the trail into coast redwood forest. Turning north, it passes homes used by personnel of the park administration and an orchard dating to earliest settlement of the area.

After crossing the bridge over Boyes Creek, hikers join Cathedral Trees Trail leading west to the park entrance. Return to the campground either along the road, or by completing the circle to Prairie Creek along Nature Trail.

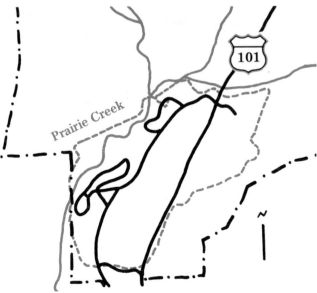

Prairie Creek

TRIP FIVE

JAMES IRVINE-MINERS RIDGE LOOP HIKE

Begins: Elk Prairie Campground.
Ends: Elk Prairie Campground.
Approximate Distance: 10.2 miles (16.4 km).
Approximate Hiking Time: 2 days.
Difficulty: Easy.
Special Equipment: Visitors overnight at Gold
                Bluff Beach Campground.
Maps: U.S.G.S. Topographic Sheets, Fern Canyon
      and Orick, Calif. N4122.5-W12400/7.5 and
      N4114-W12400/7.5
      1966.

Remarks: The route explores virgin coast redwood
          groves on historic mining trails that once
          linked Elk Prairie with camps at Gold
          Bluff beach. Hikers view enroute Fern
          Canyon, a stream-cut gorge with fern-
          covered walls, then overnight at Gold
          Bluff Beach Campground.

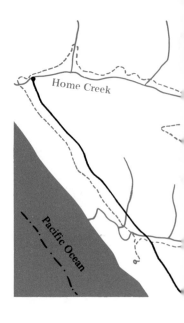

James Irvine-Miners Ridge Loop begins near park headquarters at Elk Prairie Campground. Hikers should start the walk at the marked trailhead a few feet east of the ranger station. From the starting point, follow the trail .5 mile *(.8 km)* west to Prairie Creek. For more than 1.5 miles *(2.4 km)*, the trail follows the watercourse of Godwood Creek. Hikers should watch their footing, as roots exposed by heavy use may be hazardous.

About 3.6 miles *(5.8 km)* from trailhead, the route passes a tributary of Home Creek, then enters coastal meadows before descending to Davison Road at Fern Canyon. Hikers may wish to explore the canyon before proceeding. Numerous species of ferns, including maidenhair, five-finger and sword, grow vertically from banks of the river canyon.

From Fern Canyon, follow Davison Road south along the beach 1.6 miles *(2.6 km)* to Squashan Creek, site of Gold Bluff Beach Campground. Hikers may overnight at the campground facility. Backpack camping outside designated campgrounds is not permitted in state park lands.

The following day, hikers should follow Miners Ridge Trail east along the south bank of Squashan Creek. Numerous wildlife, including Roosevelt elk, may be seen throughout the route. Such elk are largest among park wildlife, and visitors should take care to avoid them. The trail ascends through coast redwood and spruce forest to an old road bordering a forested area. About 2.5 miles *(4.8 km)* from Gold Bluff Beach Campground, the trail

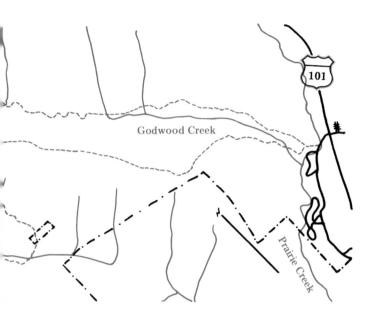

Godwood Creek

101

Prairie Creek

forks from the road and continues
southeast. After descending steeply to waters of Godwood Creek, it
joins Godwood Trail and returns
to the starting point.

TRIP SIX

WEST RIDGE-PRAIRIE CREEK LOOP HIKE

Begins: Elk Prairie Campground.
Ends: Elk Prairie Campground.
Approximate Distance: 11.5 miles (18.5 km).
Approximate Hiking Time: 8 hours.
Difficulty: Easy.
Special Equipment: During rainy periods, hikers
should wear footgear suitable
for fording creeks and swampy
areas.
Maps: U.S.G.S. Topographic Sheets, Orick and Fern
Canyon, Calif. N4115-W12400/7.5 and
N4122.5-W12400/7.5
1966.

Remarks: West Ridge-Prairie Creek Loop provides
excellent views of slope coast redwood
forest and streamside plantlife, as well as
numerous species of wildlife. Along
ridges, deer and elk may be seen, but
rodents and birds are more common.
Salmon and steelhead may also be seen in
Prairie Creek waters in season.

Hikers should begin West Ridge-Prairie Creek Loop Hike at Elk Prairie Campground park headquarters building, and visitors should walk north, crossing Prairie Creek on a park service bridge. Approximately .5 mile (.8 km) from trailhead, West Ridge Trail ascends a ridge into slope redwood forest. In spring, numerous wildflowers, including wake-robin, oxalis and fairy bells may be seen at trailside. Hikers should continue along the trail 2.5 miles (4 km) until the trail junctions with Zig Zag Trail One. Ignore the fork leading east to the highway, and follow instead the continuation of West Ridge Trail.

About 4.5 miles (7.2 km) from trailhead, hikers junction with Zig Zag Trail Two, again leading east to Prairie Creek and U.S. Highway 101. Beyond this junction, West Ridge continues 1.1 miles (1.8 km) to Zig Zag Trail Three, the final alternate. The trail passes through forested lands cut prior to establishment of the park. Hikers may either continue north along West Ridge Trail to the final alternate, or follow Zig Zag Trail Two east to begin their return to the campground.

Those continuing along West Ridge Trail to Zig Zag Three may accidently miss the final junction. Beyond, a road built during forestry of the area leads further north. Should such a mistake occur, retrace your path to Zig Zag Trail Three, first ascending steeply, then descending, to Prairie Creek.

Prairie Creek watershed has been protected for more than 30 years, and hikers may pass numerous big leaf maples, alder and

willow trees blanketed with growths of moss. In autumn, such trees become colorful with dying leaves. Along banks of the creek, visitors hiking during autumn and winter spawning periods may view steelhead and salmon. Steelhead commonly reproduce in very shallow water.

Prairie Creek Trail travels south, paralleling U.S. Highway 101 for much of its distance. Hikers must cross the creek several times on footbridges. Such bridges are occasionally removed during periods of high water, and winter and spring travelers may expect fordings.

Follow Prairie Creek Trail south 4.5 miles *(7.2 km)* to reach the starting point at Elk Prairie Campground headquarters.

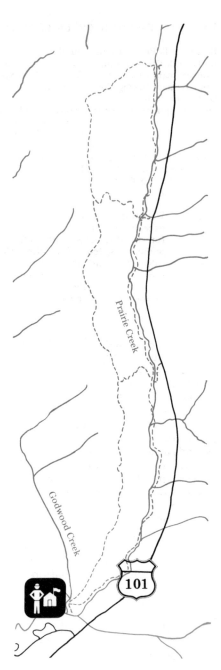

TRIP SEVEN

RHODODENDRON-FOOTHILL LOOP HIKE

Begins: Elk Prairie Campground.
Ends: Elk Prairie Campground.
Approximate Distance: 8.5 miles (13.7 km).
Approximate Hiking Time: 9 hours.
Difficulty: Easy.
Special Equipment: None normally required.
Binoculars or a camera may
prove helpful while observing
wildlife.
Maps: U.S.G.S. Topographic Sheets, Orick, Fern
Canyon and Tectah Creek, Calif.
N4115-W12400/7.5, N4122.5-W12400/7.5
and N4115-W12315/15
1966.

Remarks: The trail passes from streamside forests
of alder, big leaf maple and tanoak to
slope forests of coast redwood. In spring,
California rose-bay rhododendron color
higher elevations with colorful blossoms,
while in autumn, maples display bright
yellow leaves.

Hikers begin Rhododendron-Foothill Loop Hike at Elk Prairie Campground park headquarters. Trailhead is located a few feet east of the visitor center, and hikers first parallel the entrance road to U.S. Highway 101, then cross Boyes Creek on a footbridge. For approximately 1.2 miles *(1.9 km)*, the trail passes through aromatic groves of California laurel and big leaf maple. In autumn, fallen leaves brighten the path.

From Boyes Creek, hikers should follow Rhododendron Trail upslope into coast redwood forest. After passing a series of gullies and fallen trees, the trail enters an area of dense oxalis and ferns, made especially beautiful by their contrast with nearby large Redwood trees. Approximately 1.8 miles *(2.9 km)* from trailhead, the path joins Cal-Barrel Road.

Hikers should follow the road northeast until a footpath leads once again to northwest.

In this area, hikers may see hundreds of plants of California rose-bay, or rhododendron. In spring, such plants color the forest with blossoms of pink, red, lavender and white. Approximately 1 mile *(1.6 km)* from Cal-Barrel Road, the trail junctions with South Fork Trail, then continues to Brown Creek. Hikers should follow Rhododendron Trail to Brown Creek, then turn west along the creek on Brown Creek Trail.

About .2 mile *(.3 km)* before Brown Creek Trail joins U.S. Highway 101, hikers should turn left on Foothill Trail. The path leads south and parallels the highway to Big Tree.

Visitors may return to Elk

Prairie Campground from Big Tree either by following Foothill Trail, or by crossing the highway to Prairie Creek Trail. Both lead in .3 mile *(.5 km)* to park headquarters.

TRIP EIGHT

BROWN CREEK-C.R.E.A. HIKE

Begins: U.S. Highway 101, 3.1 miles (5 km) north
   of Elk Prairie Campground turnoff.
Ends: U.S. Highway 101, 3.1 miles (5 km) north
   of Elk Prairie Campground turnoff.
Approximate Distance: 3 miles (4.8 km).
Approximate Hiking Time: 2 hours.
Difficulty: Easy.
Special Equipment: None normally required.
Maps: U.S.G.S. Topographic Sheet, Fern Canyon,
   Calif. N4122.5-W12400/7.5
   1966.

B.E. FERNOW

Brown Creek-C.R.E.A. Hike allows visitors close examination of typical slope redwood forest. It is ideal for visitors with limited time or hiking experience. Hikers reach the starting point by traveling 3.1 miles *(5 km)* north of Elk Prairie Campground on U.S. Highway 101 to trailhead of C.R.E.A. Trail. The trail is named for a dedicated grove sponsored by the California Real Estate Association. The path departs the highway to northeast, following a seasonal stream. Approximately .4 mile *(.6 km)* from start, hikers ascend a ridge, then follow its crest south through slope redwood forest. Many California rose-bay rhododendrons grow at trailside, and walking C.R.E.A. Trail is particularly enjoyable in spring.

About 1.6 miles *(2.6 km)* from trailhead, hikers junction with Brown Creek Trail. Those wishing to extend their outing may travel east on Brown Creek Trail to Rhododendron Trail. By following reverse instructions for Rhododendron - Foothill Loop Hike, Trip Seven, visitors may return to Elk Prairie Campground. Those wishing to return to the highway should turn west on Brown Creek Trail, following the watercourse to U.S. Highway 101. Visitors should arrange vehicle pickup, as walking U.S. Highway 101 is not recommended due to heavy traffic.

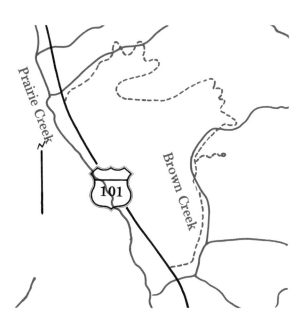

TRIP NINE

TEN TAYPO-HOPE CREEK LOOP HIKE

Begins: 5.4 miles (8.7 km) north of Elk Prairie
    Campground on U.S. Highway 101.
Ends: 5.4 miles (8.7 km) north of Elk Prairie
    Campground on U.S. Highway 101.
Approximate Distance: 4 miles (6.4 km).
Approximate Hiking Time: 3 hours.
Difficulty: Easy.
Special Equipment: None normally required.
Maps: U.S.G.S. Topographic Sheet, Fern Canyon,
    Calif. N4122.5-W12400/7.5
    1966.

Remarks: Ten Taypo-Hope Creek Loop passes
    through virgin groves of slope redwood
    forest. The trail begins 5.4 miles
    (8.7 km) north of Elk Prairie Campground
    turnoff on U.S. Highway 101. Visitors
    should park in the provided turnout,
    west of the highway. Take particular
    care to secure all valuables left in cars,
    as occasional acts of vandalism have been
    reported near this portion of park highway.

From trailhead, hikers may proceed east along Ten Taypo Trail. The route follows a seasonal stream, and winter and spring hikers may find the trail slippery when crossing marshy areas. Approximately .5 mile (.8 km) from the starting point, the trail junctions with Hope Creek Trail. Hikers should continue along the eastern fork .2 mile (.3 km) to East Ridge Road, a fire lane. Turn north on the road, descending approximately .5 mile (.8 km) to its junction with Hope Creek Trail and Lucy H. Hume Grove. For much of its path, the route passes through ridges of coast redwood forest, and many large trees may be seen.

Hikers should follow Hope Creek Trail northwest from East Ridge Road 1 mile (1.6 km). At this point, the trail once again junctions with Ten Taypo Trail. Return to the trailhead and U.S. Highway 101 by following Ten Taypo Trail south.

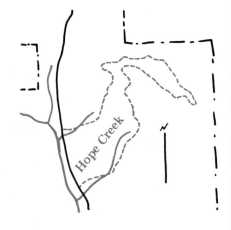

TRIP TEN

GOLD BLUFF BEACH-REDWOOD CREEK HIKE

Begins: Mile 1 (km 1.6), South Coastal Drive.
Ends: Orick gateway.
Approximate Distance: 14.5 miles (23.3 km).
Approximate Hiking Time: 2 days.
Difficulty: Moderate.
Special Equipment: Water bottle or other suitable
                 container. Sun burn preventative.
                 Hikers overnight at Gold Bluff
                 Beach Campground.
Maps: U.S.G.S. Topographic Sheets, Fern Canyon and
                 Orick, Calif. N4122.5-W12400/7.5 and
                 N4115-W12400/7.5
                 1966.

Remarks: The hike follows 13 miles (20.9 km) of
                 scenic park coastline. Hikers overnight at
                 Gold Bluff Beach Campground. Carry
                 water, as some portions are dry.

Gold Bluff Beach-Redwood Creek Hike offers backpackers a wide range of undisturbed park coastline. Included are miles of wide, sandy beach and rocky coves, as well as grassy meadows near the mouths of Butler and Squashan creeks. Hikers reach the starting point from Elk Prairie Campground turnoff by driving U.S. Highway 101 north 7.6 miles (12.2 km) to start of Coastal Drive alternate. Follow the alternate 1 mile (1.6 km) to reach the trailhead. The starting point is directly across the highway from Goddard Grove signpost and is unmarked. Hikers should descend an old road leading west towards the sea through groves of alder and Sitka spruce.

About .4 mile (.6 km) from trailhead, hikers cross Johnson Creek and enter a grassy flat over-looking Carruther's Cove. A very steep trail near the south end of the meadow leads to the beach.

At low tide, hikers may continue south along the shore 1.6 miles (2.6 km) to Ossagon Creek and road. The road is presently closed to traffic, and hikers may wish to picnic at the mouth of Butler Creek, .2 mile (.3 km) south. Both Ossagon and Butler creeks provided water during early attempts to mine Gold Bluff beach. Gold was discovered at the site in 1850, when beach shores of the park were much narrower. At that time, ocean waves frequently washed against the bluffs. Mining camps were constructed nearby, and unsuccessful attempts to gather beach riches continued until 1920. The beach has continued to widen in recent years.

Continue south to Gold Bluff

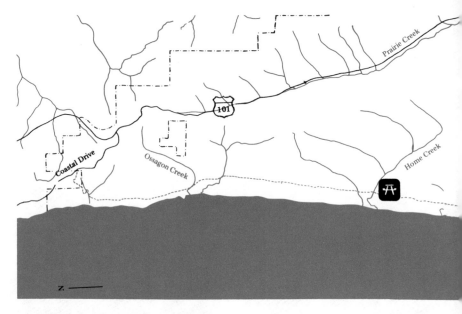

Beach Campsite, 3.7 miles *(6 km)*.
Before reaching the campground,
hikers pass the mouth of Home
Creek and Fern Canyon.   Fern
Canyon is a scenic gorge with vertical walls covered by the growth
of ferns. Hikers wishing to extend
their outing may walk John Irvine
Trail inland to Elk Prairie Campground.

Gold Bluff Beach Campground
is an open campsite with running
water and rustic facilities for seacoast travelers.   Hikers intending
overnight stays should reserve
space.   State park regulations require that all campers stay within
designated campsites.

The following day, hikers may
continue south along the beach,
following either Davison Road or
firm sand near the water edge. Approximately 1.8 miles *(2.9 km)*
south of Gold Bluff Beach Camp-

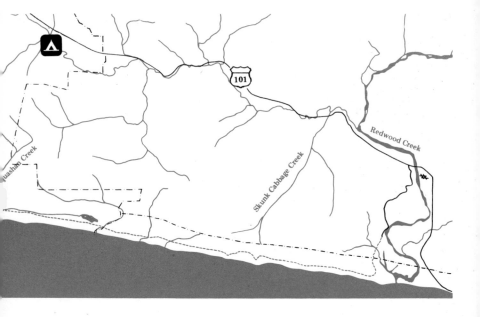

ground, Davison Road turns east to join U.S. Highway 101 south of Elk Prairie Campground. Hikers near this point pass from Prairie Creek Redwoods State Park and re-enter federal lands. Backpack camping is allowed in the intertidal zone, and personnel of the park administration request that all visitors register at the Orick gateway prior to departure. Only driftwood fires are permitted at such camps.

About 1.8 miles *(2.9 km)* south of state park boundaries, hikers must climb the bluff to avoid Mussel Point. Because heavy underbrush is common a short distance inland, remain on the bluff face, being careful to avoid undercut areas. Beyond Mussel Point 1.7 miles *(2.7 km)*, waters of Redwood Creek block further southerly travel. An access road, located .2 mile *(.3 km)* inland provides easy return along the north bank of the creek to the Orick gateway.

TRIP ELEVEN

HOBBS-WALL LOOP HIKE

Begins: Red Alder Campground.
Ends: Red Alder Campground.
Approximate Distance: 4.5 miles (7.2 km).
Approximate Hiking Time: 4 hours.
Difficulty: Easy.
Maps: U.S.G.S. Topographic Sheet, Childs Hill,
Calif. N4137.5-W12400/7.5
1966.

Remarks: Hobbs-Wall Loop Hike offers hikers close
views of alder forest and abundant wildlife.
Throughout its length, the route follows
paths used during early forestry, by steam
locomotives and sections of puncheon, or
corduroy, road.

Hikers begin Hobbs-Wall Loop Hike by following Trestle Loop Trail from Red Alder Campground in Del Norte Coast Redwoods State Park. The trail begins between campsites 7 and 8, then ascends a small slope to parallel the park road. The area surrounding Mill Creek Campground was logged early in the century, and hikers first pass through alder and second-growth redwood forest. Approximately .1 mile *(.2 km)* from start, the trail junctions with a campground access trail leading east. Hikers should ignore the path and continue to the start of Skyline Trail, leading west towards the park entrance station.

Near the entrance station, hikers must follow a short connecting trail which leads to Hobbs-Wall Trail. The trail name honors Hobbs, Wall and Company, a timber firm that operated lumber camps nearby until 1939. From the entrance station, hikers cross a footbridge leading over a seasonal stream to coast redwood slope forest. Near the park entrance, the trail follows a wagon road dating many years into park history. The road was originally paved with split redwood timbers, and approximately 1.9 miles *(3 km)* from trailhead closely passes the roadbed of present-day U.S. Highway 101. At this point, hikers may examine roadbuilding techniques, unique to redwood country. To level the roadbed, early highway engineers filled many gullies with redwood logs, sometimes to depths of 20 feet *(6 m)*. A fill of dirt and puncheon planks completed the surface. U.S. Highway 101 still follows such fills for much of its dis-

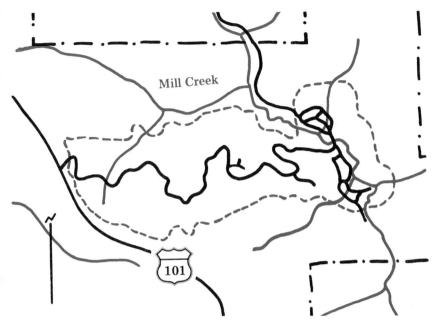

Mill Creek

101

tance within the park.

From the log crib, hikers should continue north and cross the entrance road. After descending a slope, the trail crosses a stream several times before junctioning with an old logging road. Follow the roadbed downstream until it narrows to trail width. Plants of stinging nettle are common, and hikers should be careful to avoid close contact. The plants may raise welts in sensitive individuals even through clothing.

Approximately 1 mile *(1.6 km)* from the entrance road, hikers follow the waters of Mill Creek. A short distance beyond, Hobbs-Wall Trail joins Alder Basin and Trestle Loop trails. Hikers wishing to extend their outing may follow these trails to an old steam railway trestle. Built during the logging period, the trestle once

joined main lines leading north to Crescent City.

Hobbs-Wall Trail ends at Cascara Campground. Hikers may return to their starting point by following the park road.

TRIP TWELVE

DAMNATION CREEK HIKE

Begins: U.S. Highway 101, 4.3 miles (6.9 km) south
    of Mill Creek Campground turnoff.
Ends: U.S. Highway 101, 4.3 miles (6.9 km) south
    of Mill Creek Campground turnoff.
Approximate Distance: 3.6 miles (5.8 km) round trip.
Approximate Hiking Time: 5 hours.
Difficulty: Moderate.
Special Equipment: Water bottle or other suitable
                container.
Maps: U.S.G.S. Topographic Sheets, Childs Hill and
    Sister Rocks, Calif. N4137.5-W12400/7.5 and
    N4137.5-W12407.5/7.5
    1966.

Remarks: Damnation Creek Hike passes steeply from
    stands of coast redwood forest to rocky
    seacoast. Nearly 1000 feet (304.8 m) of
    elevation loss and gain occurs in 3 miles
    (4.8 km) of horizontal distance. Hikers
    must carry water for dry portions of this
    route.

Damnation Creek Hike provides visitors with outstanding views of virgin coast redwood forest and scenic, rocky seacoast. Hikers reach the starting point by driving 4.3 miles *(6.9 km)* south from Mill Creek Campground turnoff on U.S. Highway 101. A trailhead turnout and signpost provides ample parking. Visitors planning hikes on Damnation Creek Trail should carefully secure all valuables as occasionally vandalism has been reported along this portion of the highway.

From the start, hikers ascend steeply through coast redwood forest to a gentle ridge, then begin a steep descent .3 mile *(.5 km)* from trailhead. Extremely large trees are common in this area. California rose-bay rhododendron often climb nearly 40 feet *(12.2 m)*, dotted with green leaves and pink to purple flowers. In spring, wake robin and oxalis flower colorfully on the forest floor.
climb nearly 40 feet *(12.2 m)*, dotted with green leaves and pink to purple flowers. In spring, wake robin and oxalis flower colorfully on the forest floor.

About 1.2 miles *(1.9 km)* from trailhead, hikers may view waters of the Pacific Ocean through the forest, then follow closely the path of Damnation Creek to the coast. The name of the creek may have been suggested by early settlers attempting to penetrate the dense coast redwood forest near its banks. Pioneer explorer Jedediah Smith camped near headwaters of Damnation Creek after leaving False Klamath Cove in June, 1828.

Immediately before reaching

the coast, hikers cross a footbridge leading to the beach. Damnation Cove is rocky, and visitors may enjoy observing tidepool animals or exploring a natural sea arch to the south. Avoid such exploration in times of high tide, however. Tides may trap unwary hikers for many hours.

Return to the starting point on U.S. Highway 101 by following the outbound route.

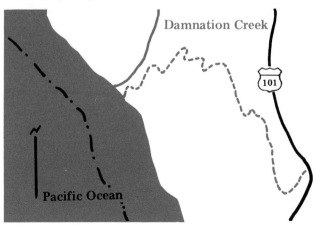

TRIP THIRTEEN

NICKEL CREEK-LAST CHANCE HIKE

Begins: U.S. Highway 101, 4.3 miles (6.9 km) south
   of Mill Creek Campground turnoff.
Ends: U.S. Highway 101, 4.3 miles (6.9 km) south
   of Mill Creek Campground turnoff.
Approximate Distance: 15 miles (23.2 km) round trip.
Approximate Hiking Time: 2 days.
Difficulty: Moderate.
Special Equipment: Hikers overnight at Nickel Creek
                   Campground. Winter hikers may
                   have to ford streams if footbridges
                   are out.
Maps: U.S.G.S. Topographic Sheets, Childs Hill and
   Sister Rocks, Calif. N4137.5-W12400/7.5 and
   N4137.5-W12407.5/7.5
   1966.

Remarks: Nickel Creek-Last Chance Hike travels
         through coastal terrain, including coast
         redwood forest, shrublands and alder forest.
         Visitors may see a wide variety of wildlife
         and plantlife. Hikers overnight at Nickel
         Creek Campground.

Hikers reach trailhead by driving south of Mill Creek Campground turnoff 4.3 miles *(6.9 km)* to the start of Damnation Creek Trail. A parking access provides ample space for automobiles. Hikers should carefully secure all valuables, however, as occasional vandalism has been reported along this portion of highway.

From trailhead, hikers should follow Damnation Creek Trail west to a signpost marking the start of Last Chance Trail. Continue along Last Chance Trail through coast redwood forest, passing headwaters of Damnation Creek. The creek was discovered by pioneer explorer Jedediah Smith in 1828.

From Damnation Creek, hikers should proceed west along the trail, passing numerous small seasonal streams and creeks. Califor-nia rose-bay rhododendron and western azalea are common in this portion of the park, and blossom during late spring with beautiful flowers of white, rose, lavender and orange.

About 4 miles *(6.4 km)* from trailhead, hikers intersect the route of power transmission lines linking Klamath and Crescent City. An access road provides easy walking much of the remaining 3.5 miles *(5.6 km)* to Nickel Creek Campground. Hikers follow the seacoast closely, and excellent views may be had of rugged coastline extending north and south. Numerous animals and birds are common, including gulls, crows, terns, chickaree and deer. Offshore, during spring and autumn, gray whales migrating north to Arctic waters or south to Baja California pass near the shore.

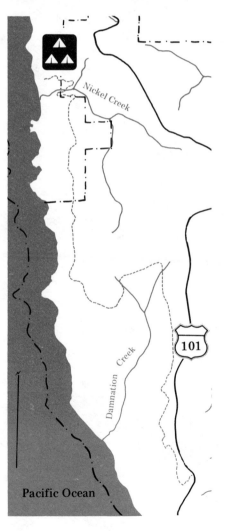

Such whales may be identified from other marine mammals by their wide, flat flukes and high spouts.

Hikers overnight at Nickel Creek Campground, a facility of the National Park Service. Chemical toilets and abundant water from Nickel Creek make this seaside camp a pleasant stay. Visitors should take care to avoid exposed headlands, however, as strong gusts of winds may prove hazardous to campers. Hikers may return to the starting point the next day by following the outbound path, or end the outing by vehicle pickup at Crescent Beach Overlook, located .5 mile *(.8 km)* north of the campground.

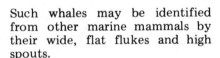

Nickel Creek

101

Damnation Creek

Pacific Ocean

TRIP FOURTEEN

COASTAL HIKE

Begins: Parking turnout, mile 2 (km 3.2), Requa Road.
Ends: Lagoon Creek Fishing Access.
Approximate Distance: 4.3 miles (6.9 km).
Approximate Hiking Time: 6 hours.
Difficulty: Easy.
Special Equipment: Water bottle or other suitable container. Binoculars or a camera may prove helpful to those wishing to closely observe sea wildlife. Hikers should carry a sunburn preventative lotion or cream.
Maps: U.S.G.S. Topographic Sheet, Requa, Calif. N4130-W12400/7.5 1966.

Remarks: Coastal Hike is the first completed section of Pacific Coast Trail. It offers hikers scenic vistas, varied bird and animal life, and plants of coastal shrublands. Visitors should carry water as stream water on this route is not potable due to salt spray. Avoid Coastal Hike during periods of strong wind.

Hikers reach trailhead by driving U.S. Highway 101 2.7 miles *(4.3 km)* north of Klamath Bridge to its junction with Requa Road. Follow Requa Road west 2 miles *(3.2 km)* to a parking turnout. The trail begins a few feet east.

From trailhead, hikers should follow the trail northwest to an overlook. From this point, numerous wave-cut terraces common to shores near the park may be seen. Sea caves are visible to north along the water edge, while upslope, hikers may see housing units of Klamath Air Force Station, a radar site. During spring and summer, visitors to Coastal Hike may see Allen's and rufous hummingbirds, extracting nectar from salmonberry thickets at trailside. For several miles, the trail passes through alder and Sitka spruce forest.

About .9 mile *(1.6 km)* from the starting point, the trail forks in several alternates used by riders on horseback. Hikers should disregard these paths, however, and continue walking north near the coast. A short distance beyond, a creek forms a pond. Hikers should not drink stream water on this route, as wind-carried salt spray renders it briny.

In many places, overlooks provide hikers with excellent views of the scenic park seacoast to west. Sea lions and seals frequently may be seen sunning themselves on exposed rocks. A short distance offshore, migrating gray whales are common in spring and autumn. Each year, gray whales travel north to Arctic waters before returning to winter breeding grounds in Baja California.

About 3.3 miles *(5.4 km)* from

trailhead, hikers pass Hidden Beach, a quiet, sandy cove suitable for picnicing or observing seashore tidepool animals. Approximately .2 miles *(.3 km)* to north of the beach, Yurok Loop Trail joins Coastal Hike. Hikers may continue .4 mile *(.6 km)* to Lagoon Creek Fishing Access by either trail.

Visitors intending travel on Coastal Hike should carry an adequate sunburn preventative. Sun and windburn, even on overcast days, are common on park seacoasts.

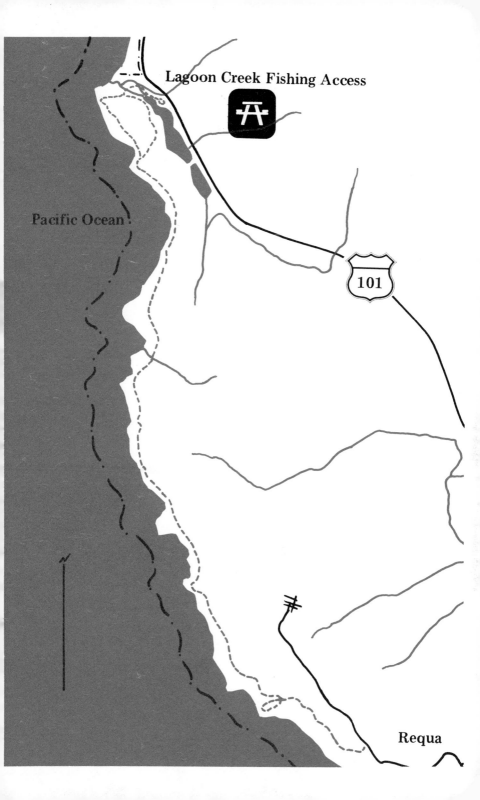

Lagoon Creek Fishing Access

Pacific Ocean

101

Requa

TRIP FIFTEEN

STOUT GROVE WALK

Begins: Smith River footbridge, Jedediah Smith
    Redwoods State Park campground.
Ends: Smith River footbridge, Jedediah Smith
    Redwoods State Park campground.
Approximate Distance: 1.8 miles (2.9 km)
    round trip.
Approximate Hiking Time: 2 hours.
Difficulty: Easy.
Special Equipment: None normally required.
Maps: U.S.G.S. Topographic Sheet, Hiouchi,
    Calif. N4145-W12400/7.5
    1966.

Remarks: Stout Grove Walk passes near the
    largest known coast redwood, Frank
    D. Stout Tree. From Stout Grove, the
    trail continues eastward along smith
    River through inland ridge forest.

Stout Grove Walk begins at the summer footbridge spanning Smith River. In winter, hikers May alternately reach the starting point by driving east from the campground to South Fork Road. Cross Smith River, then turn west on Howland Hill Road to Stout Grove parking access.

From the footbridge, hikers should walk eastward along Smith River to Stout Grove. A wooden fence placed by personnel of the park administration protects near-surface roots of the largest known coast redwood, Frank D. Stout Tree. The redwood is 20 feet (6.1 m) in diameter at chest height and rises more than 300 feet (91 m) into the air. It was named for Frank D. Stout, an early conservationist of the Save-The-Redwoods League.

From Stout Grove, hikers should continue eastward along Smith River .7 miles (1.1 km) to its junction with Howland Hill Road. Enroute, visitors may see inland ridge forest unusual to this area of the park. Included are trees of Port Orford cedar, a species found growing only in northern California and southern Oregon. From end of the trail, hikers may return to the campground by retracing the outbound route, or by following the road west to Stout Grove parking access.

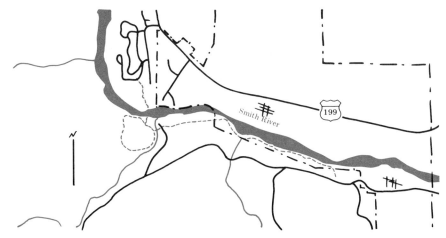

TRIP SIXTEEN

SMITH RIVER-HATTON GROVE HIKE

Begins: Summer footbridge, Jedediah Smith
      Redwoods State Park Campground.
Ends: U.S. Highway 199, 1.3 miles (2 km) west of
      Hiouchi Bridge.
Approximate Distance: 2.8 miles (4.5 km).
Approximate Hiking Time: 3 hours.
Difficulty: Easy.
Special Equipment: None normally required.
                Binoculars or camera and a
                water bottle may prove
                helpful.
Maps: U.S.G.S. Topographic Sheet, Hiouchi,
      Calif. N4145-W12400/7.5
      1966.

Remarks: Smith River-Hatton Grove Hike provides
         excellent views of both alluvial and slope forest.
         Many overlooks offer scenic vistas of Smith
         River and Hiouchi Bridge.

Hikers begin the hike at the summer footbridge leading from Jedediah Smith Redwoods State Park campground across Smith River. In winter, the starting point may alternately be reached by driving east on U.S. Highway 199 to South Fork Road. Cross Smith River on the road and turn west on Howland Hill Road until reaching Stout Grove parking access. From the starting point, hikers should follow Loop Trail west 200 yards (183 m) to its junction with Hiouchi Trail. Continue along the west bank of Smith River on Hiouchi Trail.

A short distance from trailhead, hikers cross a seasonal stream on a footbridge. During much of the year, water is spotty along the route, and hikers may wish to carry a water bottle or other convenient container. The trail ascends from alluvial stands of coast redwood common in Frank D. Stout Grove to forests typical of higher elevations. In several spots, railed overlooks provide views of Smith River and Hiouchi Bridge.

Visitors may notice the deep turquoise color of Smith River. Its distinctive hue is caused by upstream beds of serpentine rock. Such rock is formed by metamorphic deformation of sedimentary and igneous beds. About 1.3 miles (2.1 km) from trailhead, the path passes through the hollow base of a dead redwood. Such hollows are caused by fungal rot entering through a fire scar. In early days, settlers of the areas frequently used them to confine poultry and called them "goose pens."

After reaching the crest of a

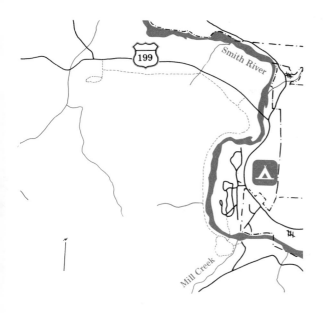

small rise, hikers junction with an access trail leading .1 mile *(.2 km)* to U.S. Highway 199 and Hiouchi Bridge. One may either return to the campground along the highway, or continue to Hatton Grove by following the west fork 1.1 miles *(1.8 km)*. The access trail to Hatton Grove follows the highway closely, a short distance upslope, and hikers are seldom distant from traffic noise.

At Hatton Grove, an access trail leads south to a loop trail passing through slope redwood forest. Hikers wishing to extend their hike may walk the .3-mile *(.5-km)* loop. From junction with the access trail, hikers should turn north to U.S. Highway 199. End of Smith River-Hatton Grove Hike is a rest area providing access to Simpson-Reed, Peterson and Skinner groves. Hikers should

arrange for vehicle pickup at this point.

Simpson-Reed--Peterson Groves Walk and Leiffer-Ellsworth Groves Walk offer alternates to hikers who wish to prolong their outing.

TRIP SEVENTEEN

SIMPSON-REED -- PETERSON GROVES WALK

Begins: Highway turnoff, 1.2 miles (1.9 km) west
of Hiouchi Bridge on U.S. Highway 199.
Ends: Highway turnoff, 1.2 miles (1.9 km) west
of Hiouchi Bridge on U.S. Highway 199.
Approximate Distance: 1.2 miles (1.9 km).
Approximate Hiking Time: 1 hour.
Difficulty: Easy.
Special Equipment: None normally required.
Maps: U.S.G.S. Topographic Sheet, Hiouchi,
Calif. N4145-W12400/7.5
1966.

Hikers reach the starting point of Simpson-Reed -- Peterson Groves Walk either by driving 1.8 miles *(2.9 km)* northwest from the campground at Jedediah Smith Redwoods State Park on U.S. Highway 199, or by hiking Smith River-Hatton Grove Hike. A turnout and rest area provides ample parking.

Hikers should proceed north from trailhead along an access trail leading 100 yards *(91 m)* to Simpson-Reed Grove. The grove was established as a dedicated grove by the Save-The-Redwoods League, in memory of Mark E. Reed, President of Simpson Timber Company, 1914-1933. Junction of the access and grove trails is marked with an interpretive sign describing events of history during the life of oldest redwoods.

Hikers should turn east from the interpretive sign, following Simpson-Reed Loop Trail. Rustic log benches provide convenient rest stops throughout the walk. Approximately .3 mile *(.5 km)* from start, the loop junctions with Peterson Loop Trail. Peterson Grove includes several small meadows where visitors may see numerous birds and small animals. From the junction, the trail continues in a loop to Clark's Creek, then turns south and crosses a seasonal stream before returning to the starting point.

Clarks Creek

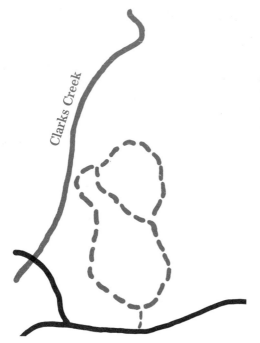

TRIP EIGHTEEN

LEIFFER-ELLSWORTH GROVES WALK

Begins: Mile .4 (.6 km), Walker Road.
Ends: Mile .4 (.6 km), Walker Road.
Approximate Distance: 1.3 miles (2.1 km)
              round trip.
Approximate Hiking Time: 1 hour.
Difficulty: Easy.
Special Equipment: None normally required.
Maps: U.S.G.S. Topographic Sheet, Hiouchi,
    Calif. N4145-W12400/7.5
    1966.

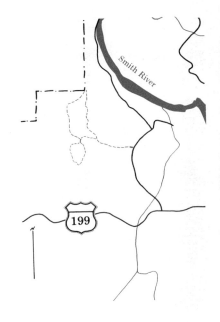

Hikers reach the starting point on Walker Road either by driving 2 miles *(3.2 km)* northwest from the campground at Jedediah Smith Redwoods State Park on U.S. Highway 199, or by following the Smith River-Hatton Grove Hike. Turn north on Walker Road, driving .4 mile *(.6 km)* to trailhead.

From trailhead, hikers should walk west through coast redwood forest until reaching a fork in the trail. Follow the west fork, leading to Ellsworth Grove. Many rustic log benches provide convenient rest stops in this scenic area, and frequent meadows break the forest. In such areas, visitors may see a wide variety of wildlife, including Stellar's jays, Townsend's chipmunks and gray squirrels.

Approximately .3 mile *(.5 km)* from start, hikers may extend their walk by turning south from the main trail on a short, .3-mile *(.5-km)* loop. Tanoak, madrone and alder are common along the diversion. Continuing from junction with the loop trail, the path leads north to Leiffer Grove. The dedicated glade honors Dorothy and Murray Leiffer, conservationists of the Save-The-Redwoods League.

Approximately .2 mile *(.3 km)* beyond junction with the loop trail leading south, hikers turn sharply south and return .5 mile *(.8 km)* to the starting point.

TRIP NINETEEN

MILL CREEK HIKE

Begins: Smith River footbridge, Jedediah Smith
Redwoods State Park Campground.
Ends: Howland Hill Road, Mile 3.5 (km 5.6)
southwest of the junction with U.S.
Highway 199.
Approximate Distance: 4.5 miles (7.2 km).
Approximate Hiking Time: 2.5 hours.
Difficulty: Easy.
Special Equipment: None normally required.
Binoculars or a camera may
be helpful while observing
wildlife.
Maps: U.S.G.S. Topographic Sheet, Hiouchi,
Calif. N4145-W12400/7.5
1966.

Remarks: Mill Creek Hike follows the watercourse
of Mill Creek upstream from Smith
River to the site of a settler's Cabin at
old Nickerson Ranch. Varied wildlife,
including heron, mergansers, water ouzel,
kingfisher, beaver, salmon and steelhead
may be seen enroute.

Hikers should start Mill Creek Hike by crossing Smith River from the campground to Frank D. Stout Grove. During winter, the starting point may alternately be reached by driving east on U.S. Highway 199 to South Fork Road. Cross Smith River and turn west onto Howland Hill Road, which leads to Stout Grove.

From the footbridge over Smith River, hikers should follow the loop trail approximately .3 mile *(.5 km)* to start of Mill Creek Trail. The trail leads south up a short rise. For 1.3 miles *(2 km)*, the path borders Mill Creek, and visitors may see a wide variety of wildlife, including many species of birds, amphibians and mammals. At trailside, many trees common to inland streams of the park become visible. Most noticible are alder, willow, tanoak and madrone. Hikers may also see signs of beaver. Such animals were transplanted to the park during World War II. They do not usually construct lodges and dams common to beaver of other areas, however.

At approximately 1.3 miles *(2 km)* from start, an access trail leads southeast to a highway bridge. Hikers may return along Howland Hill Road to Stout Grove or continue southwest 1.6 miles *(2.6 km)* to Nickerson Ranch. Enroute, the trail follows Howland Hill Road closely, crossing it several times. One mile *(1.6 km)* from the highway bridge access, the trail passes a meadow suitable for picnicing.

Nickerson Ranch was an early dwelling abandoned for many years. Few visible remains may be seen. From Nickerson Ranch,

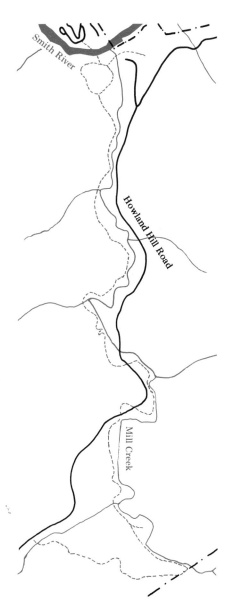

visitors should return to Howland Hill Road by following the access trail northwest .8 mile *(1.3 km)*. Near junction of trail and road, a parking area marks an access trail to Stagecoach Road. Stagecoach Road was built in 1856 by personnel of Crescent City Plank Road and Turnpike Company and is paved with puncheon timbers of split redwood. The road is visible for nearly .3 mile *(.5 km)*.

Hikers may return to camp either by prearranged vehicle pickup or by following Howland Hill Road to Stout Grove.

TRIP TWENTY

BOY SCOUT TREE-FERN FALLS HIKE

Begins: Mile 3.3 (km 5.3), Howland Hill Road.
Ends: Mile 3.3 (km 5.3), Howland Hill Road.
Approximate Distance: 6.2 miles (10 km).
Approximate Hiking Time: 5 hours.
Difficulty: Moderate.
Special Equipment: None normally required.
                      Hikers may wish to carry a
                      lunch.
Maps: U.S.G.S. Topographic Sheets, Hiouchi
        and Crescent City, Calif.
        N4145-W12400/7.5 and N4145-W12407.5/7.5
        1966.

Remarks: The trail explores outstanding coast
           redwood slope forest enroute to
           beautiful Fern Falls. Many massive
           trees and easily visible at trailside,
           including Boy Scout Tree.

Visitors reach the starting point, mile 3.3 *(km 5.3)* on Howland Hill Road, by driving east from Jedediah Smith Redwoods State Park campground on U.S. Highway 199. Cross Smith River on South Fork Road, then turn west onto Howland Hill Road. Because Howland Hill Road is narrow, vehicles more than 7 feet *(2.1 m)* wide or 20 feet *(6.1 m)* long, single or in combination, are not recommended. The starting point may also be reached on foot by following Mill Creek Hike to its end. From end of Nickerson Ranch Trail, hikers should walk Howland Hill Road northeast .2 miles *(.3 km)* to trailhead.

From the starting point, walk northwest along the trail. A small creek, located approximately .3 miles *(.5 km)* from trailhead provides a convenient water stop

the footbridge, hikers follow a stream flowing west, then ascend a steep ridge.

About 2.8 miles *(4.5 km)* from the starting point, the trail forks. Hikers wishing to visit Boy Scout Tree should follow the upslope trail 30 yards *(27.4 m)*. From the fork, hikers who wish to continue to Fern Falls should follow the main trail leading west.

After following the course of Jordan Creek for .5 mile *(.8 km)*, the trail turns sharply northward. A short distance beyond, Fern Falls tumbles in several cataracts. Hikers may picnic near the falls, but open fires should be built only on gravel bars of the stream. Always extinguish such fires completely before returning to the starting point.

A wide variety of wildlife may be seen near Fern Falls. Included

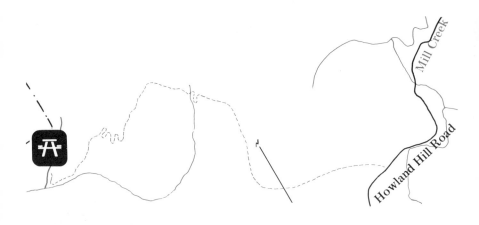

are birds such as chestnut-backed chickadees, Stellar's jays and Allen's hummingbird. Deer sometimes visit Jordan Creek in early morning hours. Also common are gray and Douglas squirrels.

TRIP TWENTY-ONE

SMITH RIVER FLOAT

Begins: Jedediah Smith Redwoods State Park
Campground.
Ends: U.S. Highway 101 bridge.
Approximate Distance: 8.4 miles (13.5 km).
Approximate Time on River: 8 hours.
River Rating: Class I.
Season: May - June.
Fishing: Small trout in river year-round.
Excellent steelhead and salmon in
late summer and fall.
Maps: U.S.G.S. Topographic Sheets, Hiouchi
and Smith River, Calif.
N4115-W12400/7.5 and N4152.5-W12407.5/7.5
1966.

Remarks: Hikers float from Jedediah Smith Redwoods
State Park to U.S. Highway 101 on smooth,
lazy water that is warm in summer. Ideal for
families or groups with little river rafting
experience.

Smith River watershed drains the rugged Siskiyou Mountains to east of Jedediah Smith Redwoods State Park. Upstream from the park, both north and south forks of Smith River provide challenging whitewater to river enthusiasts. From the park, and downstream, however, visitors may enjoy quiet floating through scenic countryside, pleasant swimming, and picnicing on river bars.

Floaters should put in at the campground picnic area. Below Hiouchi Bridge, North Bank Road parallels the river nearly to U.S. Highway 101. Floaters soon pass out of protected state park lands and into forested areas owned by timber and lumber companies.

When floating Smith River, watercraft users should allow for summer upstream winds in afternoon. Such winds may be both strong and chilling. A sweater, or other protection, is advised. Safety precautions, including good swimming ability and life preservers are also recommended. Boils, eddies and snags in mid-river may otherwise concern floaters.

Upon reaching the highway bridge spanning Smith River, floaters should leave the river. Arrange for vehicle pickup before departing Jedediah Smith Redwoods State Park.

TRIP TWENTY-TWO

KLAMATH RIVER FLOAT TRIP

Begins: Weitchpec, Calif.
Ends: U.S. Highway 101, Klamath River Bridge.
Approximate Distance: 38 miles (61 km).
Approximate Time on River: 2-3 days.
River Rating: Class I and II.
Season: February - November.
Fishing: Excellent trout, salmon and steelhead
      fishing in nearly all larger creeks. Deeper
      holes and riffles may yield larger trout or
      steelhead.
Maps: U.S.G.S. Topographic Sheets, Klamath, Ship
      Mountain, Tectah Creek, Coyote Peak and
      Hoopa. N4130-W12400/15, N4130-W12345/15,
      N4115-W12345/15, N4100-W12345/15, and
      N4100-W12330/15
      1952.

Remarks: Klamath River Float Trip offers miles of
      scenic waterway rich in beauty and wildlife.
      Although the river is rated Class I and II
      water, it is not recommended to those at-
      tempting first trips. For those with limited
      time, the trip may be made in one long day.

Floaters reach the put-in point at Weitchpec by traveling first U.S. Highway 101 south to its junction with U.S. Highway 299, then 299 east to Willow Creek. Floaters should then turn north on U.S. Highway 96, traveling through Hoopa Valley to Weitchpec. Floaters may alternately start the trip by traveling Klamath River upstream by jet boat from Requa.

From the put-in, Klamath River is broad and swift, even during periods of low, summer water. Many strong eddies, boils and, near confluence of Trinity and Klamath River, one Class II rapid demand attention and prior river experience. The Class II, or Thule Rapid, is located approximately 6 miles *(9.7 km)* downstream from Weitchpec. It consists of a long series of rollers with occasional breaking waves. Floaters may ap-

proach the rapid at any point, but mildest channels occur near the east bank.

Although Klamath River Float may be made in as short a time as one day, most watercraft travelers will enjoy exploring side creeks and river bars. During late spring and early summer, excellent trout fishing occurs in most larger tributaries. In autumn, floaters may angle for salmon and steelhead.

A wide variety of wildlife is also common near the river. Many birds, including great blue heron, merganzer and osprey, are abundant. Rarely, travelers may see bald or golden eagles fishing river waters. Quiet approaches may reveal black bear or deer. Near Klamath Glen, occasional sea lions and otter fish for candlefish and steelhead.

Many areas near streamside are

currently being forested by private timber operators. Visitors should never go ashore near logging areas, as such activity presents serious hazard to safety. Tree-falling is best viewed from mid-channel.

Upon reaching U.S. Highway 101 bridge spanning the river, watercraft travelers should depart the river near the northern approach. Arrange for vehicle pickup prior to departure.

TRIP TWENTY-THREE

REDWOOD CREEK WHITEWATER TRAIL

Begins: Stover Ranch, Redwood Valley.
Ends: Orick, Calif.
Approximate Distance: 28 miles (45 km).
Approximate Time on River: 3 days.
River Rating: Class II - V.
Seasons: March - April, October - November.
Fishing: Generally poor in main river. Some
    small trout in tributary creeks.
Maps: U.S.G.S. Topographic Sheets, Orick,
    Rodgers Peak, Coyote Peak, Calif.
    N4115-W12400/7.5, N4107.5-W12400/7.5,
    and N4100-W12345/15
    1966, 1966 and 1952.

Remarks: Redwood Creek Whitewater Trail offers
    experienced watercraft users an oppor-
    tunity to sample a wide variety of redwood
    country. Only those with highly maneuver-
    able craft and ample experience should
    attempt this route.

Whitewater enthusiasts may reach the put-in point at Stover's Ranch by driving south of the park on U.S. Highway 101 to its junction with U.S. Highway 299. Continue east on 299 until Redwood Valley Turnoff is reached. Stover Ranch, located at the end of Redwood Valley Road, borders the stream. All potential floaters wishing to put in at this point should request permission in person at the ranch house.

From the put-in, Redwood Creek drops swiftly through nearly 20 miles *(32.2 km)* of remote canyon. Contact with parties other than whitewater enthusiasts during this section is unlikely, and watercraft travelers must be prepared to handle any potential medical problems encountered.

Redwood Creek Whitewater Trail is ideally divided into three unequal sections: Stover Ranch to national park boundary, national park boundary to Tall Trees Grove, and Tall Trees to Orick. The first section is consistantly Class I and II-rated water. Floaters also encounter two Class III rapids which should be scouted. Most hazards concern stumps, trees and snags in channel areas. Seldom do such obstacles require more than a wide birth or low bridge, but river travelers should keep sharp lookout downstream.

End of the first section is proceeded by a long, shallow field of boulders and a sharp turn to right. At this point, a log jam nearly breaches the stream, and floaters should crowd the left bank to avoid contact. A gravel bar immediately downstream provides an excellent first night camp.

The following day, floaters

enter the second, and most difficult section of Redwood Creek. From national park boundary, the river drops rapidly into Devil's Canyon, an extremely arduous stretch of Class V water. Logs and snags sometimes straddle the creek bed, complicating downstream progress. Even very experienced watercraft users should portage this section of stream.

The first portage must be made on the left bank upstream from a waterfall 6 feet *(1.8 m)* high. Watercraft may be lined through this area. Experienced boatsmen may run Class III rapids which follow but should portage the second falls on the east side. The final, and most difficult, waterfall occurs 100 yards *(91 m)* downstream. All boaters should portage the area. Currents and eddies downstream from the falls are deceptively violent, and floaters should proceed some distance downstream before again entering the river. Portaging these waterfalls and rapids will require three to seven hours, depending on group size.

Downstream from the final portage, watercraft travelers must traverse a final Class III rapid before entering flat, wide river 3 miles *(4.8 km)* above Tall Trees Grove. Hikers should camp the second night on river bars near the grove.

The final section of Redwood Creek is comprised almost totally of flat water. Boatsmen may drift quietly downstream to Orick, then depart the river.